D1356227

TRADE UNIONS AND PRESSURE GROUP POLITICS

# Trade Unions and
# Pressure Group Politics

TIMOTHY C. MAY
*Senior Lecturer in Politics*
*Manchester Polytechnic*

 SAXON HOUSE | LEXINGTON BOOKS

*Published by*

SAXON HOUSE, D.C. Heath Ltd.
Westmead, Farnborough, Hants., England.

*Jointly with*

LEXINGTON BOOKS, D.C. Heath & Co.
Lexington, Mass. USA

ISBN 0 347 01058 X

Printed in Great Britain
by Unwin Brothers Limited
The Gresham Press, Old Woking, Surrey
A member of the Staples Printing Group

# Contents

# Preface

This book is an attempt to test some of the conclusions of earlier writers about the role of trade unions as pressure groups in the light of the experience of the last fifteen years. As such it is heavily dependent upon those earlier works and on those who have contributed to our stock of information about the British trade union movement since 1960. Though certain primary sources have been used, the aim of the book has been more directed at attempting a synthesis of the material that is already available and at indicating where more research is needed.

In addition to my debt to those writers who have advanced our knowledge and understanding of recent trade union history there are a number of other institutions and individuals whose help it is a pleasure to acknowledge. Any study of this kind is dependent upon the resources and co-operation of libraries and I have been well served in this respect by the Manchester Polytechnic Library and the Manchester Central Reference Library. I am also indebted to the Governors of Manchester Polytechnic who granted me a sabbatical term which helped considerably at an important stage in the writing of this book.

I am especially grateful to David Jary and Michael Moran who have read parts of the manuscript and contributed many suggestions for its improvement. A number of other colleagues, notably Stephen Bristow, Andrew Gray, John McHugh and Michael O'Neill have also helped in a variety of ways.

As with any empirical work on British politics one is grateful for the co-operation of those who are active in the institutions one is studying. In this respect I would like to thank John Monks of the Trades Union Congress, W.A. Brown of the Labour Party, and a number of civil servants who helped me with various queries.

Finally, I would like to thank Mrs Maureen Nugent for her extremely conscientious work in typing my manuscript.

None of the foregoing should be implicated in any way in the final product for which I am solely responsible.

Timothy May<br>
April 1975

# 1   The Study of Trade Unions and Pressure Group Politics

It would be impossible to argue that trade unions have been neglected as a field of academic study. G. S. Bain and G. B. Woolven have recently compiled a bibliography in which they list some 15,000 items and these are 'industrial relations' items and appertain only to Britain.[1] The term 'industrial relations' is worth noting for it is an illustration of the general point that academics study human behaviour from particular perspectives and that such perspectives can crystallise research so that some aspects of behaviour receive less attention than they deserve. This would seem to be the case if one examines the contribution of political scientists to the study of British trade unions. Historians have probably contributed most to our knowledge of British trade unions, broadly in three main kinds of study. First, any work devoted to the nineteenth century gives some space to describing the unions. Typically the authors link the development of modern trade unionism with the development of industrial capitalism and then go on to describe the different stages of development (e.g. New Model and New Unionism). The second type of approach is illustrated by the author who chooses to focus upon the Labour Movement or more specifically the trade unions; some of the best known and most widely acclaimed works fall into this category.[2] The third type of approach is the most specialised, taking the form of a history (in whole or part) of a particular union or group of unions. This final category is probably the most variable so far as the quality and therefore permanence to the serious student is concerned.[3]

All three of these approaches inevitably provide the political scientist with much information that is important to him. There is, for example, a discussion in the works dealing generally with the nineteenth century and in those dealing specifically with the Labour movement of the important legislative changes that governed legitimate trade union activity, as well as a discussion of the rise of the Labour Party. Nevertheless, some important developments, particularly as one moves into the twentieth century, do not seem to have received the attention they deserve — it is generally agreed that trade unions become 'accepted' and recognised by government but there has been little detailed discussion of this process. The sociologist has also contributed to our knowledge of trade unions but the potential of his discipline does not seem to have been fully developed, possibly because of the extensive influence exercised by Michels and his 'Iron Law of Oligarchy'. This concept has been responsible for the diversion of a good deal of research effort into establishing whether the 'Law' holds as Michels suggested and, if not, what are the key variables in determining its operation.[4] Some very interesting work has been produced by sociologists on the attitudes and orientations of individual trade unionists but this has tended to be a side product of other concerns.[5]

The contribution of political scientists has been minimal, at least until very recently. Despite the highly atypical organic relationship between the trade unions and the Labour Party very little was known about how this worked until the publication in 1960 of Martin Harrison's *Trade Unions and the Labour Party Since 1945*. This was — and indeed remains — a most valuable contribution to the understanding of British politics. It represented a substantial gathering of information about the political behaviour of trade unions and provided a detailed documentation of the major axes around which the relationship between the Party and the unions revolved. It demonstrated conclusively that some of the cruder stereotypes of both the trade unions and the constituency Labour parties were incorrect and showed how both changed their alignment over time and sometimes according to particular issues within the same time period. Thus Harrison's contribution is to provide a very detailed record of the relationship between trade unions and the Labour Party between 1945 and 1959 and to furnish a set of analytical perspectives with which to interpret the many events of the last fifteen years. But some major controversies within the Labour Party in which the trade unions were necessarily involved developed in the year that Harrison's book was published, for example, the debate about Clause Four and the dispute over defence policy (the opening stages of which Harrison was able to note). Equally, we have now also had the experience of six years of majority Labour government and the reconsideration of policy that followed the defeat of that government in 1970.[6]

Harrison's work on the relationship between the unions and the Labour Party was complemented in the same year by Victor Allen's *Trade Unions and the Government*.[7] As its title implies, this was an examination of the different kinds of relationship between trade unions and various governments: the trade unions as a pressure group in Whitehall; trade unions as negotiators when the government is the employer; the unions' relationship with the Labour Party when it is in power; and the attitude of government to strikes. The focus is mainly historical but, like Harrison, Allen also

2

makes some analytical contributions. Although he has subsequently written on trade unions, Allen has not attempted a major revision of the original work. As with Harrison we shall draw on some of the perspectives he provides to examine some of the events of the period under study.

Though political scientists have of course paid more attention to pressure groups than to trade unions, the study of the former is still relatively recent. W.J.M. Mackenzie is often credited with awakening political scientists to the need to study what became in the post-1945 period a phenomenon of growing importance.[8] The first book-length treatments followed three years later: S.E. Finer wrote a general survey of interest groups and J.D. Stewart focused on one of the major strategies pursued by groups in his study of their relationship to Parliament.[9] The Americans had written about pressure groups in their own country somewhat earlier (in fact one of the seminal works on this subject dates from before the First World War [10]) and a number of them were to make important substantive and theoretical contributions to the study of British pressure groups. Harry Eckstein published his study of the BMA in 1960 and this was valuable not only as a study of an important professional group but also in setting the study within an explicit theoretical framework.[11] Five years later S.H. Beer published his major work on British politics, which added to what was by now a considerable body of knowledge about pressure groups, and set this empirical work within an illuminating historical framework of different views about representation in Britain. [12]

Though a variety of terminology is employed, most students of interest groups in Britain have chosen to divide 'the group universe' into two broad categories derived by distinguishing between the objectives pursued by different groups. On this basis there is a category of what are variously termed 'sectional', 'interest' or 'spokesman' groups and another of 'cause', 'promotional' or 'ideas' groups. Typically, most professional, business and union groups find themselves included in the first category. They are groups with a permanent organisational structure established to provide certain services for their members. This may well involve them in political activity since it will be one of the main ways in which they can protect and further their members' interests.) The second category is more heterogenous since, while is does include groups which have a long history and a clearly structured organisation, it is also concerned with groups which come together to pursue some particular cause or idea — they do not reckon to provide benefits, at any rate of a material kind. Once such ideas or causes triumph — often in the form of legislative changes — such groups may well fade away or need to rejuvenate themselves by adopting fresh ideas or causes. Castles has sought to illuminate the different membership bases of the two groups. He argues that the first category has an 'objective' base — one can readily see the 'constituency' the group should aim to encompass — whereas the second broad category contains groups who need a 'subjective' identification for people to belong to them — one needs to *feel* that capital punishment or fox hunting or liberalising abortion are important issues in order to join the relevant groups. [13]

Castles further argues that Eckstein's theoretical contribution, although valuable, was limited in its applicability, being rather less useful when applied to subjective groups. He also felt that the emphasis of group studies had been too concentrated on the objective groups and insufficiently on the subjective groups. Since trade unions clearly constitute an objective group his strictures about Eckstein need not detain us but it is worth making the point that, at any rate in Britain, though many of the studies carried out in the 1950s and 1960s were of objective groups neither business nor trades unions were adequately considered. After a pioneering article on one of the peak organisations of business by Professor Finer, fifteen years elapsed before the area was re-examined. [14] Similarly, following the publication of the studies of Allen and Harrison very little was published on the political activities either of individual unions or of the TUC. [15] More recently, however, there have been some signs of a re-awakening with the work of Irving Richter and G.A. Dorfman. [16] Richter is particularly interested in the political orientations of individual unions and selected the AUEW for an extended case study, his main concern being to test how far Selig Perlman's thesis (first published in the 1920s) can illuminate the political behaviour of that union. Dorfman's book is a study of the attempt to arrive at an incomes policy at four different periods between 1948 and 1967 and owes a lot in its approach to Beer's work.

The study of elites in Britain has also come to life again after having been more or less dormant during the 1960s. [17] A number of these studies are of considerable interest to any student of the political involvement of trade unions [18] but it is still worth noting that business and commercial leaders have received far more attention than has the trade union leadership (Victor Allen's study of Arthur Deakin being the lone exception [19]). One should also note some fresh interest in the role of union sponsored MPs — a number of studies already mentioned have some bearing on this but another American, William Muller, has gone beyond many of the questions that interest elite analysts to focus on the *behaviour* of these MPs. He is interested in how far they respond to the policy positions of the unions as opposed to the dictates of the Party whip (where there is, as happened increasingly during the 1960s, an opposition between the two). [20]

It is a principal aim of this study to try to take account of this recent work on trade unions within an overall perspective of studying the strategy and tactics of trade unions as political pressure groups. This emphasis on the strategy and tactics has been advocated in R.D. Coates' study of teachers' unions. [21] He argues that inadequate attention has been paid to the distinction between *behaviour* and *influence* in many studies of interest groups. Influence is a notoriously difficult concept for political scientists to handle since it often demands knowledge that is difficult or impossible to come by and involves complicated exercises in trying to weight the activities of the various interested parties and groups. We cannot escape it entirely even if, as in this study, we choose to emphasise behaviour, for in attempting to understand and explain behaviour it is very likely that perceptions of where influence can best be deployed, or has been in the past, will enter into the explanation. Nevertheless, the question of what a person's perceptions are of where and how to exercise influence is *not* the same question as where and how influence was actually exercised and the first should be easier to answer than the second.

As a result of his study Coates emphasises that an adequate explanation of the behaviour of teachers' unions can only be given by emphasising *both* the structure of decision making — the environment that groups have to work within — and their organisational characteristics. [22] Many previous studies of groups have tended to emphasise one of these main variables to the exclusion of the other. The attempt is made in this study — particularly when discussing the role of the TUC — to pay attention to the organisational variable, for this must be one important factor in any reconsideration of the conclusions arrived at in some of the earlier works that have been discussed.

At least three kinds of organisational change can be distinguished which bear on the role of trade unions as pressure groups. Changes in the occupational structure have considerably affected many trade unions. Some of the most important unions in both the TUC and the Labour Party lost members very rapidly during the 1960s — the mineworkers, the railwaymen and the textile workers being among the most obvious examples. By contrast, other occupational sectors that grew rapidly were not, in many cases, well unionised. A good deal of discussion took place in the early 1960s concerning this phenomenon of occupational change and its implications for the trade union movement in general and the TUC and the Labour Party in particular. It was pointed out that if people were not recruited rapidly enough into what were weakly unionised areas to replace the loss in strongly unionised sectors, then there was a danger to the general position the unions had acquired and a real possibility that they would increasingly come to be seen as a minority cult. [23] George Bain in a detailed examination of trade union membership between 1948 and 1964 concluded that 'whether the British Labour movement stagnates or expands in the second half of the twentieth century will largely depend upon its willingness and ability to organise white-collar employees. [24]

The 1960s also saw a considerable debate within the trade union movement on their role. George Woodcock's famous question to the 1962 Congress — 'What are we here for?' — has often been used to illustrate this self-examination. It has revolved around a number of issues such as the structure of trade unions, the role of officials and shop-stewards and inter-union disputes. Although some of the more radical suggestions such as proposals for re-structuring the movement on the basis of 'industrial' unionism were rejected, a considerable number of union amalgamations have taken place and more are still in prospect. The TUC has been important in promoting and assisting change in many of the areas just indicated [25] and its own structure and functioning has been one of the important issues in the general debate about the purpose and direction of trade unionism. Changes in the environment, many of which are discussed in fuller detail in the following chapter, have given a strong impetus to this examination of the role of the TUC and its relationship to its affiliates. We shall pay particular attention to this issue when we examine incomes policies.

The final kind of change worth noting is one in the political orientation of some of the major unions. This change is sufficiently familiar not to need great elaboration. Harrison's analysis was important in pointing out that the orientation of unions could change, the most remarked upon changes being those associated with the two biggest unions, the TGWU and the AUEW, but it is worth noting that the TUC's sixth biggest affiliate, the EETU/PTU has changed in the reverse direction. In Harrison's analysis of union attitudes to the Labour Party's National Executive (which at the time was normally supportive of the parliamentary leadership), it was numbered among the 'consistent left' category but since the accession to the leadership of Leslie Cannon and Frank Chappell it has moved right away from that position.

The organisation of this study is as follows. In chapter 2 we shall consider in what sense the trade unions can be said to have objectives which involve them in political action and suggest that events, or the environment (to use Coates' term), has steadily politicised them during the past fifteen years. In the following three chapters the range of strategies that unions have utilised will be considered individually. The attempt will be made to demonstrate how both the organisational and environmental factors have affected these strategies. Finally, we shall attempt to draw the threads of the discussion together and to sketch some alternative scenarios for the immediate future.


## Notes

[1] The bibliography is cited in G.S. Bain and H.A. Clegg: 'A Strategy for Industrial Relations Research' (*British Journal of Industrial Relations,* vol. 12 [1], March 1974).

[2] Sidney and Beatrice Webb: *A History of Trade Unionism* (Longman, London 1894). G.D.H. Cole: *A Short History of the British Working Class Movement* (George Allen and Unwin, London 1927, revised edition 1948).

[3] G.S. Bain and G.B. Woolven: 'The Primary Materials of British Industrial Relations' (*British Journal of Industrial Relations*, vol. 9 [3], 1971, p. 393). Noting the variable quality of such histories, they comment that 'at their worst, and most of them are, they are largely primary sources: the author is either a serving or retired union official, the union retains editorial control and the resulting publication is little more than a collection of primary documents which tend to cast the union in a good light.'

[4] For the most recent summary of this kind of work see J.A. Banks: *Trade Unionism* (Collier Macmillan, London 1974) Part 3.

[5] The Affluent Worker studies are one obvious example: see particularly J.H. Goldthorpe, D. Lockwood, F. Bechhofer and J. Platt: *The Affluent Worker: Political Attitudes and Behaviour* (Cambridge University Press, London 1968).

[6] Harrison himself has contributed a chapter on 'Trade Unions and the Labour Party' to R.H. Kimber and J.J. Richardson (eds): *Pressure Groups in Britain* (Dent, London 1974) in which he examines the relationship between the two in the 1960s and early 1970s.

[7] V.L. Allen: *Trade Unions and the Government* (Longman, London 1960).

[8] W.J.M. Mackenzie: 'Pressure Groups in British Government' (*British Journal of Sociology*, vol. 4 [2], 1955).

[9] See S.E. Finer: *Anonymous Empire* (Pall Mall, London 1958) and J.D. Stewart: *British Pressure Groups* (Clarendon Press, Oxford 1958).

[10] Arthur F. Bentley: *The Process of Government*, originally published

in 1908, reprinted in 1967 by The Belknap Press of Harvard University Press, Cambridge, Mass.

[11] H. Eckstein: *Pressure Group Politics* (George Allen and Unwin, London 1960).

[12] S.H. Beer: *Modern British Politics* (Faber, London 1965).

[13] F.G. Castles: *Pressure Groups and Political Culture* (Routledge and Kegan Paul, London 1967). It should be noted that Castles himself does not use the terms 'objective' and 'subjective' groups.

[14] S.E. Finer: 'The Federation of British Industries' (*Political Studies* vol. 4 [1], 1956) and W.P. Grant and D. Marsh: 'The Confederation of British Industry' (*Political Studies*, vol. 19 [4], 1971).

[15] There was a spate of reformist literature published during the early 1960s but not only was most of this normatively orientated, it was also mainly concerned with problems of membership and structure. See William McCarthy: *The Future of the Unions* (Fabian Society, London 1962).

[16] Irving Richter: *Political Purpose in Trade Unions* (George Allen and Unwin, London 1973) and G.A. Dorfman: *Wage Politics in Britain* (Charles Knight, London 1974).

[17] In this respect W.E. Guttsman's *The British Political Elite* (Macgibbon and Kee, London 1963) can be regarded as the end point of a series of studies mainly carried out in and covering data up to the 1950s.

[18] Of particular interest are R.W. Johnson: 'The British Political Elite 1955/1972' (*European Journal of Sociology*, 1973); John Ellis and R.W. Johnson: *Members from the Unions* (Fabian Research Series, London 1974); and Victor Hanby: 'A Changing Labour Elite: The National Executive Committee of the Labour Party 1900-1972' in Ivor Crewe (ed.): *British Political Sociology Year Book*, vol. 1, 'Elites in Western Democracy' (Croom Helm, London 1974).

[19] V.L. Allen: *Trade Union Leadership* (Longman, London 1957). Tony Lane's *The Union Makes Us Strong* (Arrow Books, London 1974) gathers together some of the evidence we do have and also draws on interviews with trade union leaders – see in particular chapters 6 and 7.

[20] W.P. Muller: 'Union – MP Conflict: An Overview' (*Parliamentary Affairs*, vol. 26 [3], Summer 1973); and 'Trade Union Sponsored Members of Parliament in the Defence Dispute of 1960–1' (*Parliamentary Affairs*, vol. 23 [3], Summer 1970).

[21] R.D. Coates: *Teachers' Unions and Interest Group Politics* (Cambridge University Press, London 1972), p. vii.

[22] Ibid p. 115 *et seq.*

[23] McCarthy, op cit. and the PEP Study 'Trade Unions in a Changing

Society', the fruits of which appeared in a number of PEP broadsheets, e.g. no.463, *Trade Union Membership* (July 1962), no.472, *Trade Unions in a Changing Society* (June 1963), and no. 477, *The Structure and Organisation of British Trade Unions* (December 1963).

[24] George Sayers Bain: 'The Growth of White-Collar Unionism in Great Britain' (*British Journal of Industrial Relations* vol. 4 [3], November 1966, p. 331).

[25] D.H. Simpson in a study of trade union size in three consecutive five year periods (1954–9; 1959–64; 1964–69) noted that the degree of concentration was most marked in the last of the three periods, following the passage of the Trade Union (Amalgamation) Act of 1964. He comments on the latter: 'It can only be surmised that TUC pressure helped to pass the Act and that TUC persuasion made unions follow paths to a more ordered structure' ('An Analysis of the Size of Unions' *British Journal of Industrial Relations*, vol. 10 [3], November 1972).

# 2  Trade Unions and their Objectives

Many discussions of trade union objectives take as their starting point the Webbs' statement that trade unions are 'continuous associations of wage earners for the purpose of maintaining or improving the conditions of their working lives'.[1] Subsequent discussion has emphasised that in view of the development and rapid growth of non-manual unions the reference to wage earners needs now to be interpreted to include salary earners. But some suggestions have also been made that the definition represents too narrow an interpretation of what trade unions are about in contemporary Britain. These suggestions arise because whether one focuses on formal constitutional statements by the unions or on their actual behaviour as organisations, the Webbs' definition does not seem sufficiently encompassing. There are at least two supplementary points that should be made. Firstly, it does not take adequate account of the fact that the determination of wages and working conditions can only be partly accomplished within the framework of collective bargaining; secondly, unions appear to be concerned with many matters other than wage determination, particularly when they are collectively giving voice at the TUC Annual Congress or at the Labour Party's Annual Conference. Both these considerations point to a need for unions to engage in political activity, that is, activity designed to persuade by a variety of means the public, political parties and governments that particular action is either desirable or otherwise. Governments are by far the most important of these targets since it is they who have the authority to introduce legislation or alter administrative practice. The unions' interest in political parties and the public are simply ways of organising to assume government (in the case of the former) or rather more amorphously attempting to create a particular climate of opinion which will influence governments (in the case of the latter). It will be clear that we are hereby defining political activity by reference to the means selected by the unions for achieving particular objectives, rather than attempting *a priori* to label particular objectives as 'political' or 'industrial'.

Trade unions have been engaged in political activity in the sense of the above definition for over one hundred years. During this time three kinds

11

of concern seem to have compelled political activity. Of primary importance has been the legal framework within which trade unions have had to operate. Some of the best known trade union campaigns and indeed some of the most important political actions, such as the eventual decision to support the idea of a Labour Representation Committee, can be related to their concern for their basic legitimacy. A second concern arises through an awareness of the limitations of collective bargaining with employers. While the financial terms under which men work is rightly regarded as being at the heart of collective bargaining, the physcial and social conditions under which they work have also been a most important part of the bargaining process. But unions have long realised that the scope for achieving the conditions they consider appropriate is limited; health and safety standards are examples of areas where unions have concluded that legal enforcement is essential and this involves them in trying to persuade governments to pass the appropriate legislation. The third main concern which has impelled political action is distinguished from the second category more by a difference of degree than of kind. Again, it starts from an awareness that the control that can be exercised over union members' work situations is limited within the scope offered by collective bargaining. The limitations result from the impact of politically determined economic and social policies. Thus decisions on the levels of public spending, on employment policy, on tariffs and on the provision of social welfare all impinge upon the lives of trade unionists. If trade unionists are to attempt to exercise control over these decisions they must seek to participate in the political process by which they are determined.

So far as the legal framework of trade union activity is concerned five major campaigns have been waged since the formation of the TUC in 1868. The establishment of the Royal Commission on Trade Unions in 1868, its report and the subsequent legislation of 1871 and 1875 formed the first of these campaigns. The period from 1890 to the outbreak of the First World War was a particularly hectic period for trade unions encompassing the employers offensive in the 1890s[2] and culminating in the Taff Vale judgement of 1901. This greatly strengthened the nascent Labour Representation Committee (LRC) and the resultant Trade Disputes Act of 1906 secured a highly satisfactory settlement (from the union point of view) with a legal framework within which trade unions could operate with considerable protection. Their political activity through the Labour Party (as the LRC became known in 1906) was threatened by the Osborne Judgement of 1909 and the campaign to reverse this, resulting in the passing of the Trade Union Act in 1913, marks the third major campaign the unions had to fight. The repeal of the Trade Disputes Act of 1927, passed in the wake of the General Strike, was a constant objective of the trade union movement in the remainder of the inter-war period but it was not until the post-war Labour Government came to power that it was repealed. The most recent major campaigns have been to preserve the *status quo* which was established by the 1946 Act and thus to protest against both the Labour and Conservative Governments' desire to alter this framework. The Labour Government's proposals were successfully opposed in 1969 though the precise responsibility of the trade union movement in this abandonment is difficult to estimate. What is rather more clear is the trade union role in relation to the Conservative Government's Industrial Relations Act of 1971 – it was unsuccessful in preventing its parliamentary passage but highly successful in obstructing the day to day working of the Act.

What these five major campaigns demonstrate is that whether the initiative comes from the employers using the courts to obtain unfavourable verdicts or whether from governments presenting Bills to Parliament, the unions needed to organise a political opposition. The trade unions have had to resort to a range of tactics designed to prevent the intended passage of legislation or to persuade the Labour Party to reverse unwelcome legislation. Precisely what strategy and tactics have been adopted has been a function of the general political context in which they have found themselves and the degree of internal strength and unity they have been able to achieve. Thus before the rise of the Labour Party the unions had to attempt to work through sympathetic MPs, whether Conservative or – as was more usual – Liberal. Once a separate Labour Party developed it was able to use its bargaining strength to oblige Liberal Governments to pass legislation negating the effects of unfavourable judicial verdicts, as in 1906 and 1913. After the 1927 and 1971 Acts, union energies were directed to committing the Labour Party to a repeal of the offending legislation at the earliest opportunity and in both cases these efforts were successful. Public campaigns were also resorted to in 1927 and 1971 – though, at least in the latter case, the motive appeared to be the education and mobilisation of the TUC's own membership rather than any real hope that 'public opinion' would be influenced or influential.

We have distinguished the unions' interest in various aspects of the social and physical conditions that are attached to their members' work situations as a second major area of concern that has necessitated political activity. Health and safety questions have already been cited and others that have been important are connected with training opportunities and contracts of employment. The unions have consistently sought to persuade successive governments to assume responsibilities in many of these areas and, once successful, they maintain, mainly via specialised departments at the TUC, a constant surveillance on the operation of the appropriate legislation. Such surveillance is necessary, for technology is constantly bringing about new processes, many of which carry health and safety risks. Thus while pneumoconiosis is a well known and long established health hazard for coalminers, it has lately been joined as a major area of concern by the more recently discovered hazards attached to working with rubber and asbestos. A substantial part of the work of the TUC's Social Insurance and Industrial Welfare Committee (and the appropriate department in Congress House) is concerned with issues of this kind. This is one of the areas where links with the appropriate government departments are particularly important and valued since the prospect of legislation is likely to depend upon creating and sustaining an awareness that action is both necessary and practicable. Following the report of the Robens Committee on Safety and Health at Work[3] the Government agreed to one of the report's main proposals — that there should be a new semi-autonomous authority to supervise the whole field of safety and health at work. Although there was some argument about the composition of this new body, its establishment[4] represents something near the ideal for successful pressure group activity directed at the political and administrative executive. The Safety and Health Commission which has been established has a strong trade union representation and the full-time chairman is a former union General Secretary. Unlike many of the Advisory Committees on which trade unionists are represented, the Commission is an executive body and therefore in a position not just to keep its areas of responsibility under surveillance and make recommendations, but also to act upon them.

It is when we come to examine the third main concern which has necessitated political activity that we can see most clearly the 'politicisation' of unions that has proceeded with increasing pace since 1945. Two examples can be mentioned here. In the years preceding the Second World War the TUC had been very much aware of the inadequacies of State provision in the field of social and unemployment insurance and it was influential in persuading the Coalition Government to establish an inter-departmental committee under Sir William Beveridge to review the area in 1942.[5] The permanent official who headed the TUC's Social Insurance Department worked closely with Beveridge and the outcome was a report[6] which on Beveridge's own admission was little different from the proposals of the TUC.[7] The implementation by the post-war

Labour Government of various of the Beveridge proposals has meant a continuing concern by the TUC with the principle and the detail of insurance and welfare provisions by the State, which are now designed for all the population and often involve matters of major political controversy. Thus, starting from a concern with the situation of their own members when they are ill or unemployed, the TUC's success has resulted in an extensive state provision of social welfare. The type of provision and the way in which it is to be financed can no longer be of marginal or peripheral concern to politicians and the TUC must necessarily be drawn into highly political debates if it is to exercise a continuing influence on the type and scale of provision.

As with social welfare so with many other areas of economic and social policy where post-war British governments have extended their areas of responsibility, often with the support and encouragement of the trade unions. How far the unions have foreseen some of the implications of this greater degree of state involvement is less clear, particularly if we examine the second of our examples — the commitment to full employment. This was enunciated in a Coalition Government White Paper in 1944. The Paper's oft-quoted first sentence read: 'The Government accepts as one of their primary aims and responsibilities the maintenance of a high and stable level of employment after the War'.[8] The discussion that followed this statement of principle may not have equalled its simplicity and clarity and there may have been justifiable doubts as to how such a declaration was to be implemented;[9] nevertheless, even if the record in the ensuing thirty years had been disappointing, the White Paper would still have been significant as a major shift in the extension of state responsibility. It was an indication that people could now legitimately expect government to maintain a high level of employment; as Richard Rose has put it: 'In the 1920s and 1930s virtually no-one expected the Government to solve unemployment by economic intervention. Today both politicians and voters expect this'.[10] It means that any suggestion of a radical alternative approach to employment policy — such as that offered by Enoch Powell or Sir Keith Joseph[11] — which involves — or appears to involve — the State *willing* a higher level of unemployment has a very difficult case to make.

The record on employment however has *not* been disappointing, certainly if judged by the standards that prevailed in the inter-war period. The trade union movement has greatly benefited from this, both in terms of its own growth and in the undoubted strength it has brought to the market position of labour. But from the point of view of governments it has meant that one of the central economic problems it has had to wrestle

15

with has been inflationary pressure. Economists may dispute the balance between 'cost-push' and 'demand-pull' pressures that contribute to this inflation but few politicians, be they Conservative or Labour, have been prepared to absolve labour of some share in the responsibility. Hence trade union pressure to maintain full employment policies has evoked a continuing concern by politicians with the level of wage settlements. This has not been welcomed either by individual trade unions or by the TUC, committed as they are to the view that wages are a matter to be decided by free bargaining between employers and employees. There has been a further complication also brought about by the success of the unions in achieving certain of their basic objectives; the post-war Labour government greatly enlarged the public sector of the economy by various acts of nationalisation which resulted in an increasing number of the work force being employed either directly by government or indirectly by local authorities and a variety of *ad hoc* agencies. This development has meant that many employees are actually bargaining with the government and its agents. Given the continuing attempts of governments to contain inflation they have understandably felt that this concern must be reflected in the level of wage settlements they are prepared to sanction in the public sector. Even where they have not explicitly tried to use the public sector to de-escalate wage settlements, wage negotiations have inevitably become more politicised. [12]

But governments have not, of course, been content simply to express concern at the level of wage settlements or to try to influence private employers by placing limitations on the public sector. They have felt it necessary to establish various kinds of machinery to try explicitly to influence the level of settlements or to examine particular wage and salary awards, and to pronounce on their general compatibility with government policy. The establishment of the Council on Productivity, Prices and Income in 1956 and of the National Incomes Commission in 1962 serves as an example of these two aims respectively. Neither of these bodies received much support from the unions and thus governments found themselves resorting to more direct intervention, culminating in the first statutory wage freeze in July 1966. This precedent, first established by a Labour government, was followed by the Conservatives six years later with a similar freeze in November 1972. Both these freezes had been preceded by unsuccessful attempts to arrive at satisfactory voluntary wage restraint and both were succeeded by forms of statutory control over the limits of wage and salary awards. Similarly the various 'planning' agencies that have been established, for example, the NEDC, and its associated EDCs, have sought to involve the unions. Particularly where such

16

machinery has been established by Conservative governments, this has posed some awkward dilemmas for the trade union movement for, though it is committed to 'planning', the latter's conception of what this involves is obviously different from that of a Conservative government. But the unions have been unable to find sufficient agreement within themselves either to wholly embrace the machinery or to adopt a root and branch opposition.

The NEDC was a response to the feeling that developed during the early 1960s that what came to be called 'stop-go' policies of managing the economy were unsatisfactory and ought to be replaced by more long range and systematic economic management. But one of the reasons for the resort to 'stop-go' was the need for an attempt to check inflationary pressures and to deal with deficits on the balance of payments that resulted from these. So, although the approach was rather different from incomes policy, the establishment of the Council has to be seen as another attempt to deal with wage inflation. The NEDC was not very successful in this respect and has had to try to work out an alternative rationale for itself in subsequent years. When a voluntary agreement on a wages and prices policy failed to emerge from the Council in 1963/64 the Labour government that assumed office in October 1964 removed the discussions from its framework and the Declaration of Intent that was signed in December 1964 was achieved through separate discussions.

What seems hard to deny when one reviews the relative failure of incomes policies is that one of the conclusions which Conservative and Labour governments alike drew from the experience was that the position of the trade unions needed altering. Thus we return to what we distinguished as the first concern that had impelled the unions to political action – the law which provides the basic framework for their activities. Obviously it would be an over-simplification to suggest that there was a direct relationship between the failure to arrive at an agreed incomes policy and the efforts of the Labour government in 1969 and the Conservative government in 1970/71 to alter the law governing trade union activity. But many of the other elements that one would need to take account of (e.g. the growth of unofficial strikes and demarcation disputes), were analysed in a similar manner to the incomes problem: that trade unions have strengthened their effective power and now have a capacity to obstruct the achievement of objectives that politicians have been perpetually concerned with – a favourable balance of payments, the containment of inflation, economic growth, and stable prices. The attempts to change the law have proved unsuccessful, but neither this experience nor the difficulties of incomes policy have shifted the

17

conviction of politicians that some kind of regulation of incomes remains a central political issue.

The Labour Party have sought to approach the problem afresh by means of what is variously termed a social 'compact' or 'contract'. What is interesting about this from the point of view of our general argument is that it represents a further politicisation of the unions. The Labour Party, after its defeat in 1970, was concerned to rebuild its fractured relationship with the unions. This was greatly facilitated by the nature of the Conservative government's policy, especially its Industrial Relations Act. A central part of trade union strategy in opposing this was to extract a promise from the Labour Party that a future Labour government would repeal the Act in its entirety as a matter of priority. Its agreement to do this led to co-operation between the Parliamentary Labour Party (PLP) and the TUC in opposing the parliamentary passage of the Bill and the subsequent formation of a Liaison Committee to discuss wider areas of policy. From the discussions of this Committee a bargain or contract began to emerge, the essence of which was that in response to various legislative promises on economic and social policy the trade unions would exercise a degree of self-restraint on incomes.

If policy making in the Party was the prerogative of the PLP and if one could ignore the role of the Liaison Committee, the Annual Conference and the NEC, there is little doubt that the PLP would have adopted many of the same policies which did come to constitute Labour Party policy between 1970 and 1974. But the fact that the Liaison Committee came to occupy such a central part — at least in relation to economic matters — and that the policies were presented as part of an exchange deal with the unions, made them appear to be the most important policy making section of the Party. [13] Furthermore, to have *any* chance of success in maintaining its side of the bargain, i.e. to exercise wage restraint, the TUC would have to constantly pressurise the government to honour its legislative promises and would expect to be in close continuous contact on matters both of principle and detail.

Two further points are worth making about the social contract. Firstly, it has given trade unions the opportunity to take the initiative and not simply to react to policies initiated elsewhere. Thus the defensive and negative aspects of trade union political action which have necessarily dominated its approach to the legal position of the unions are less in evidence and the unions have the opportunity to propose policies which they are anxious to see given legislative enactment. This enables the unions, at least in principle, to make more headway with some of their policies which are less directly related to the traditional union areas of

18

wages, working conditions and the legal framework governing their activities. Thus the demands for a substantial increase in the Old Age Pension which have been particularly pressed by the TGWU and adopted as general TUC policy have been accepted by the Labour Party as a top priority, down to the precise monetary amount asked for by the TUC. The second point is that the contract has been negotiated with the TUC and highlights one of the developments that we shall need to examine in more detail at a later stage. The kind of political role that the social contract envisages for trade unions has been negotiated with the TUC and this is bound, as most of the previous incomes policy experiments have been, to bring a renewed emphasis on the potentialities and limitations of united trade union action through its major representative body.

To summarise the argument of this chapter, the discussion began by suggesting that political action involves activities that are designed to persuade the public, political parties and, most important governments that some kind of legislative or administrative action either should be undertaken or, where such proposals are thought to be hostile to union interests, refrained from. On the basis of this definition three broad concerns were identified which have impelled unions into political activity. The first and most fundamental was a concern with the broad legislative framework which establishes the legal parameters for trade union behaviour. Trade unions have normally found themselves in the past one hundred years reacting to initiatives from two main sources — the proposals of politicians and the judgement of the Courts. In both cases the unions have seen their existing rights challenged or threatened and have been forced to wage campaigns in the attempt to conserve existing rights. Where they have been unsuccessful (as with the 1927 Trade Disputes Act or the 1971 Industrial Relations Act) they have concentrated on committing a future Labour government to reverse the offending legislation as a matter of priority.

It was argued that beyond this fundamental concern with legal status, union involvement in politics could be seen as deriving from an awareness of the limitations of the collective bargaining situation. The distinction was made between matters which were fairly closely connected with the conditions of work (for example, health, safety, re-training) which tended to concern only trade unionists, and areas such as fiscal and taxation policy, the regulation of demand and prices and incomes policies, areas which affect all members of society and are matters of major political controversy. In either case, though, the claim was made that the acceptance or accommodation of trade union demands has tended to politicise the unions. What is meant by this is that unions become drawn into the administrative and political apparatus, firstly in order to pursue these objectives and secondly to help supervise their operation. Social insurance and full employment were discussed at some length in order to illustrate this process. In the case of the latter the successful implementation of full employment policies has strengthened the market position of labour. Many politicians and civil servants have seen a connection between this and inflation and thus have devoted a lot of time since 1945 in trying to contain wage pressures through an agreement with the TUC for voluntary restraint. Whether a statutory policy has been in operation or not, governments have regarded the level of wage settlements as a central component in economic policy making. As part of their effort to avoid statutory curbs or to try to make them more palatable, governments have attempted to meet other union objectives in the fields of economic and social policy. Through this process unions have had the opportunity to operationalise some of their constitutional commitments to an alternative social and economic and indeed political order. Unions may wish to be left to bargain collectively with employers within a favourable legal framework [14] but post-war British governments, with their concern about incomes and their steady expansion of the State's responsibilities, have made this very difficult to maintain. Whether trade unions are seriously committed to an alternative order or not, governments have wanted to know from them the price to be paid for (at the minimum) a voluntary restraint on incomes. In their desire to maintain wage determination without governmental or legal interference unions have found it impossible to *escape* from political involvement.

## Notes

[1] Sidney and Beatrice Webb quoted in N. Robertson and K.I. Sams (eds): *British Trade Unionism* (Basil Blackwell, Oxford 1972), vol. 1, p. 42.

[2] This is usually understood to mean the combination of unfavourable judicial verdicts and political action by the employers' organisations.

[3] In July 1972. For a summary of its main recommendations see *TUC Report 1972*, pp. 128–30.

[4] It was established with the passage of the Health and Safety at Work Act in 1974.

[5] See Angus Calder: *The People's War* (Jonathan Cape, London 1969), p. 525.

[6] *Social Insurance and Allied Services*, CMD 6404, 1942.

[7] Lionel Birch: *The History of the TUC, 1868–1968* (TUC, London 1968), p. 126.

[8] CMD. 6527 *Employment Policy* (HMSO 1944).

[9] Donald Winch suggests this in a most illuminating discussion of the White Paper *Economics and Policy* (Hodder and Stoughton, London 1969), pp. 267–73.

[10] Richard Rose: *Politics in England Today* (Faber and Faber, London 1974).

[11] *The Guardian* of 6 September 1974 contains a full report of a speech by Sir Keith Joseph in which he questioned various aspects of economic orthodoxy in the post-war period.

[12] Two of the post-war Conservative Governments have tried to use the public sector to de-escalate pay claims and awards (1961; 1970/71). On the latter occasion it is interesting to note that, in response to TUC complaints that it was discriminating against the public sector, the Government replied that it had 'said no more and no less to chairmen of nationalised industries than it had said to private employers but the Government's position as banker to the public sector meant that it could not help but be more directly involved' (*TUC Report 1971*, p. 273).

[13] The social contract was given a central place in the Labour Party's election campaign in October 1974.

[14] As Irving Richter (op.cit.) has argued in the case of the AUEW.

# 3 The Relationship between the Trade Unions and the Labour Party

In considering trade unions as interest groups the vote at the 1899 Trades Union Congress to support the establishment of a Labour Representation Committee was an excellent example of pressure group behaviour. The experience of the 1890s indicated that the environment the trade unions were working in had become more difficult. The difficulties arose out of the more aggressive action by employers and a series of unfavourable judicial verdicts, which in retrospect can be seen as a trailer for the Taff Vale judgement of 1901. The employers were adopting more hostile industrial tactics and had formed an Employers Parliamentary Council in 1898 to oppose the TUC's Parliamentary Committee and to campaign for 'free contracts and free labour'.[1] Equally, the trade unions were undergoing internal change as the number of active socialists within them increased, particularly in the new unions which had grown considerably from the 1880s onwards.[2] Thus one must see the support of the TUC in 1899 for an independent body to sponsor working class candidates as a response to a situation in which industrial action appeared to be insufficient to pursue traditional trade union objectives. It cannot be seen as a commitment to an alternative social order and the LRC and subsequently the Labour Party had no coherent programme or philosophy until the adoption of a constitution in 1918. Individual trade union affiliation was far from overwhelming — it required the Taff Vale judgement to spur many unions into affiliation but some major unions which had been well placed to obtain parliamentary representation through the Liberal Party still held back (the miners, for example, did not affiliate until 1909).

The socialist commitment of the Labour Party is usually seen as the complement to its new organisational coherence deriving from the constitution adopted in February 1918. Beer is often associated with this point of view and he points to the considerable growth of trade union membership during the First World War arguing that 'the adoption of the new ideology (i.e. socialism) was not so much a cause as an effect of the

23

hardly avoidable break with the Liberals'.[3] This suggests that, as McKenzie has subsequently argued,[4] one should treat with more scepticism than Beer himself does the significance of this conversion to a socialist ideology. The evidence suggests that, so far as trade unions were interested in the 1918 constitution, it was the organisational rather than the ideological aspects that concerned them. Allen quotes an extract from Beatrice Webb's Diaries in which she reports the views of Tom Shaw of the United Textile Factory Workers Association. Shaw was worried that the control previously exercised by the trade unions might slip away under the terms of the new constitution and that it would enhance the role of the 'ambitious middle class politician ... and missionary intellectual'.[5] While one might think these fears were exaggerated, given the overwhelming predominance of the trade unions on the NEC, it certainly was the case that the middle class element in the Party increased from 1918 onwards.[6] Perhaps rather more significant for emphasising that the Labour Party and the trade unions were far from being the same body under two different labels was the experience of the two minority Labour governments in 1924 and 1929–31. Whatever allowances may be made for their minority status, in both cases they consistently emphasised that the unions were one, and only one, interest among many which had to be taken into account. The concepts of 'responsibility' and 'national interest' were deployed to ensure that the unions could not expect the Labour administration to respond solely to their demands. Indeed it is the experience of these governments that gives rise to the feeling that in some important respects Labour governments are more difficult to deal with than Conservative ones. Labour ministers (particularly at this time when they were often ex-trade union officials) claimed to *know* from their own experience what the unions would want and hence formal consultation with the TUC was deemed to be unnecessary. At its most charitable this may explain why Ramsay Macdonald told Sidney Webb when appointing him as Minister of Labour in 1929 that he could obtain a legislative programme from Sir Alan Smith, a leading employer's representative.[7] One of the main factors that strengthened the dislike of Fred Bramley, the then General Secretary of the TUC, for the shared departments of the TUC and the Labour Party (established in 1922) was this neglect of consultation by the first Labour government. The departments in fact only survived for a brief period after this and their disappearance is a further small, but not insignificant, sign of structural separation.[8]

After the 1931 financial crisis which brought to an end the second minority Labour government the trade unions re-asserted their control over the Labour Party. Henry Pelling describes the Party in the period

1931—40 as 'the General Council's party',[9] and Ernest Bevin became a key figure within the Party, important both in disputes about the leadership and in policy determination. The experience of the majority Labour government from 1945—51 was a great deal happier than that of the inter-war administrations so far as the trade unions were concerned. Basically this resulted from a successful bargain between the unions and the government. The Labour administration reversed the 1927 Trade Disputes Act as one of its first measures, nationalised certain basic industries [10] and developed economic and social programmes which fulfilled various objectives of the TUC. [11] The TUC for their part responded to the government's appeal for wage restraint in 1948 and gave general support to the government — a number of the large unions combined to protect the leadership at Labour Party conferences from criticism. But one should note here that there were a number of important developments which bode less well for a continuance of this mutually satisfactory relationship. In the first place access to Whitehall departments had been extended during the war and this was confirmed by post-war practice — unlike the experience after the First World War. Thus the unions had direct access to departments and to ministers over and above their position within the Labour Party. Secondly, the Labour Party, or rather the PLP that emerged from the 1945 General Election, displayed a distinctively different profile from that of its pre-war counterpart. Trade union sponsored MPs had comprised one half of the PLP elected in 1935 but this proportion dropped to less than a third in 1945, and Guttsman notes that teachers had ousted miners as the biggest single occupational grouping in the PLP. [12] Although at Cabinet level those with a working class background and a career as trade union official were as strongly represented in 1950 as when Attlee formed his initial Cabinet five years before, the underlying direction of change was unmistakable and by the time Harold Wilson formed his first Cabinet in 1964, less than a third could claim this pedigree against more than half in the Attlee cabinets. [13] No relationship between political views and class or occupational background is assumed in giving these details; they are cited only to demonstrate that an inevitable consequence of them was a growing feeling of separate identity between the unions and the PLP. The clearest example of the former identity between the two was Ernest Bevin. He had spent all the inter-war years as the leader of the biggest British trade union and he had occupied a key place on the General Council of the TUC. In the post-war Labour Cabinet he held the major office of Foreign Secretary almost until the government was defeated in the 1951 General Election. No comparable figure has emerged in the post-war period — Frank

Cousins' inclusion in Wilson's first Cabinet may have been an attempt to follow this precedent but it failed after only a short period. The final important point about the 1945—51 experience, which indicates a changing relationship between trade unions and the Party was that, despite the inclinations of the union leadership to continue support for wage restraint in 1950, it was made impossible by rank and file resistance in the wake of rising prices. Only by risking a substantial loss of support and a consequent threat to their own leadership could their support have continued. In any case, even had they been prepared to take this risk, it would have been of doubtful utility, since the policy depended upon voluntary compliance by the membership.

Nevertheless, at least up until the mid-fifties, major unions such as the TGWU, and NUM, and the NUGMW under the respective leadership of Deakin, Lawther and Williamson continued to cast their votes in a way that supported the leadership and opposed the Bevanite challenge that developed after the 1951 Election. With the death of Arthur Deakin and his replacement as General Secretary by Frank Cousins (following a very brief interregnum under W. J. Tiffin), it became clear that the bond between the parliamentary leadership and a sufficient number of major unions to protect that leadership had been broken. Both the controversy over Hugh Gaitskell's attempt to modify Clause Four and that over defence policy in the 1959—61 period highlighted the difficulties the Labour Party constitution gave rise to, especially in opposition, when the parliamentary leadership and the major trade unions were in disagreement. This was particularly difficult for Gaitskell and his allies since the view that its trade union and working class image needed to be modified was an important part of their analysis of the problems of the Labour Party at that time. But what the Clause Four and defence disputes demonstrated was that the trade unions were exercising a most important role in determining the outcome of both issues. Gaitskell's reversal of the 1960 unilateralist decision (albeit again very evidently due to switches of support among major trade unions), the difficulties of the Conservative government and the growing prospect of an election combined to strengthen the position of the parliamentary leadership. Harold Wilson's accession to the leadership in 1963 brought a great difference in leadership style if not in policy orientation. Wilson has consistently aimed at maximising party unity, blurring possible personality and policy conflicts. He chose to concentrate on the themes of economic growth and the technological revolution which appeared to by-pass some of the traditional conflicts and the Party was able to win a narrow victory in October 1964.

It soon became apparent, however, that some of the awkward questions which were implied by the Party's commitment to a 'national incomes policy' had not been faced in opposition but would now have to be confronted by a Labour government and that they were likely to make for difficult relations with the trade unions. [14] The record of events is examined in rather greater detail in the following chapter but there is no doubt that by the time Wilson called an election in June 1970, trade union/Labour Party relations were only just recovering from one of the worst, perhaps *the* worst, crises they had suffered since the formation of the LRC in 1900. The statutory intervention in collective bargaining to try to secure an incomes policy and the attempt to revise the legal framework governing trade unions were the main factors responsible. With the defeat of the Party the leadership was in an extremely vulnerable position so far as its control over policy and the NEC and the Party Conference was concerned. Since incomes policy and the White Paper *In Place of Strife* [15] had been abandoned while Wilson and the Labour Cabinet had had the authority that accrues to those who hold executive office, it was hardly conceivable that any attempt to challenge the role of the unions when out of office would have stood much chance of success. Furthermore, so far as *In Place of Strife* was concerned they could not escape the fact that substantial sections of the PLP had resisted the policy and that the result of the election made a policy of accommodation rather than confrontation a major priority while in opposition.

The unions for their part might have been inclined to withdraw from Labour Party involvement but the Conservative government's actions, particularly the Industrial Relations Act, made this unlikely. It was true that a number of unions both urged, and engaged in, a programme of direct action to fight the Conservatives' proposals but the majority of unions favoured the more orthodox course of obtaining a commitment from the Labour Party to repeal in its entirety the Conservative legislation when they next came into office. It was not particularly surprising that from the initial contacts between the TUC and the Labour Party to plan opposition to the Industrial Relations Bill the discussions should have widened to embrace other economic and social policies. But, equally, it is difficult not to feel that the parliamentary leadership had less to give and a greater need for trade union co-operation, and the trade unions correspondingly more to offer the PLP while having less need for its support. As Eric Heffer, one of the unions' strongest sympathisers within the PLP has put it: 'Labour is nothing without the trade unions but the trade unions can survive without the Labour Party'. [16]

In order to examine the relationship between the trade unions and the

Labour Party it is proposed to look in rather greater detail at the following aspects: (i) the sponsorship of MPs by trade unions; (ii) the role of the trade unions at the Annual Conference and in the National Executive Committee (NEC) of the Labour Party; (iii) the financial contribution of the trade unions to the Party; and (iv) some general considerations about the contemporary character of the trade union movement and the Labour Party. These areas have been chosen for examination partly in the light of the earlier analysis of Harrison and partly because the information that is needed to test some of the earlier conclusions is fairly readily available. The focus for these four sections will be on developments during the past fifteen years or so and it is hoped that this approach will amplify the very general sketch of the relationship between the unions and the Party that has been given above.

## Trade union sponsorship of MPs

When Martin Harrison reviewed the record of trade union sponsorship up to the 1959 General Election he came to a number of broad conclusions. [17] So far as the continued strength of the trade union sponsored element of the PLP was concerned he was not optimistic. Despite the success of individual unions (e.g. the AUEW) in increasing their representation, he saw the trade union and working class elements as losing strength. The unions were to some extent to blame for this as they were unimaginative in their approach to parliamentary representation, preferring to concentrate upon safe seats and offering the type of candidate who was frequently at a disadvantage when competing with better educated, younger, and frequently middle class rivals. Nevertheless, Harrison recognised that with the opportunities opened up by the Whitehall relationship it could validly be asked why trade unions bothered at all to maintain sponsorship. Broadly, he thought that the provision of specific benefits through using sponsored members was less important to the unions than a generalised desire to ensure that the atmosphere and outlook of the Party should continue to be influenced by working class thought and reaction.

The data available indicates that, contrary to what might have been predicted from Harrison's analysis, the trade unions have maintained their position over the last fifteen years. Their share of Labour Party candidates has in fact remained remarkably constant throughout the post-war period, varying only by a very small percentage (see Table 3.1). Similarly, after slumping badly in 1945, [18] the size of the trade union sponsored group in relation to the PLP as a whole has varied only a little, reaching its post-war maximum in February 1974 (see Table 3.2).

28

## Table 3.1

### Trade union sponsored candidates at general elections, 1929–74

|  | 1929 | 1931 | 1935 | 1945 | 1950 | 1951 | 1955 | 1959 | 1964 | 1966 | 1970 | 1974 (Feb.) | 1974 (Oct.) |
|---|---|---|---|---|---|---|---|---|---|---|---|---|---|
| Total | 137 | 142 | 130 | 124 | 137 | 136 | 127 | 129 | 138 | 138 | 137 | 155 | 140 |
| Percentage of all Labour Party candidates | 24 | 29 | 24 | 21 | 22 | 22 | 20 | 20 | 22 | 22 | 22 | 24 | 22 |

## Table 3.2

### Trade union sponsored MPs, 1929–74

|  | 1929 | 1931 | 1935 | 1945 | 1950 | 1951 | 1955 | 1959 | 1964 | 1966 | 1970 | 1974 (Feb.) | 1974 (Oct.) |
|---|---|---|---|---|---|---|---|---|---|---|---|---|---|
| Total | 114 | 35 | 78 | 120 | 111 | 108 | 95 | 92 | 120 | 132 | 114 | 127 | 128 |
| Percentage of all Labour Party MPs | 40 | 76 | 51 | 31 | 35 | 37 | 34 | 36 | 38 | 37 | 40 | 42 | 40 |

## Table 3.3

### The contribution of individual unions to the trade union sponsored group of MPs at selected points, 1929–74

|  | 1929 | 1945 | 1955 | 1966 | 1974 (Oct.) |
|---|---|---|---|---|---|
| NUM | 37 | 29 | 36 | 20 | 14 |
| TGWU | 11 | 14 | 15 | 20 | 17 |
| NUGMW | 7 | 8 | 4 | 8 | 10 |
| NUR | 7 | 10 | 8 | 5 | 5 |
| TSSA | 6 | 7 | 5 | 4 | 2 |
| USDAW | 3 | 7 | 10 | 6 | 4 |
| AUEW | 3 | 3 | 6 | 13 | 12 |
| NUPE | – | – | – | 4 | 5 |
| ASTMS | – | – | – | 1 | 9 |
| Others | 26 | 22 | 16 | 19 | 22 |
| Total | 100 | 100 | 100 | 100 | 100 |

Sources:    1929–59 Martin Harrison op.cit.

1964–70 Labour Party Annual Conference Reports, 1964, 1966 and 1970

1974 Assistant National Agent of the Labour Party

Within these overall totals, however, the contribution of individual unions shows a good deal of change. If one takes the thirty year period since 1945 a number of clear trends emerge (Table 3.3). Industrial sectors where employment has contracted and the corresponding unions have lost strength have also seen their position undermined within the trade union group. Coalmining and the railways — with the NUM, the NUR and the TSSA as the principal unions involved — contribute a declining share of both candidates and MPs. In contrast, the two largest unions in Britain, the TGWU and the AUEW, have both increased their representation, especially during the 1960s. The AUEW offers the most striking increase: from four MPs in the 1945 Parliament they doubled their representation in 1950, then maintained that position until doubling again in 1964, although their numbers have remained constant since then. The TGWU had a larger base from which to expand and, although there were some signs of decline in the 1950s, these were sharply reversed in the 1960s and they replace the NUM as the union with the largest group of sponsored members in 1974. The only other union to sponsor ten or more successful candidates for more than one election [19] has been the NUGMW. From ten members in 1945 it declined steadily in the 1950s and had only four sponsored MPs at the beginning of the 1959 Parliament. But it has since regained all its former strength and now has more sponsored MPs than ever before.

Two final developments since 1945 can be discerned, both of which reflect changes in the pattern of employment and consequent growth of the relevant unions: NUPE, which has grown from a membership of 150,000 in 1948 to 470,000 in 1973, has started to sponsor candidates and has had considerable success — a total of six MPs by 1970, and three white-collar unions — ASTMS, APEX, and TASS, all of which expanded considerably during the 1950s and 1960s — have also shown an interest in sponsorship and numbered twenty-one successful candidates between them by October 1974. [20]

However, if we go beyond the aggregate figures and examine the *kind* of candidates the various unions have been prepared to sponsor some considerable differences emerge. The AUEW and the NUGMW represent polar opposites in some respects. The former was one of the first unions to break away from the various traditional methods used by the unions for selecting a panel of candidates to receive a sponsored status. Though there was some variation in these methods, in principle they all assumed that a willingness to stand for Parliament and an endorsement by some section of the membership were sufficient grounds for selecting candidates for financial assistance; [21] the AUEW's innovation was to institute tests to establish suitability above and beyond the individual's own inclinations and to reinforce placement on the parliamentary panel with regular periods of political education. This has been subsequently identified as one of the main strategies by which unions can maintain their hold on parliamentary seats, which power — it will be recalled — Harrison thought was threatened by the unions' unimaginative approach to sponsorship. [22] Although this approach can clearly be called meritocratic it has not resulted in the union's rank and file being squeezed out, in fact quite the reverse. The paid union official, possibly advancing in years, who has been seen as the characteristic trade union MP is virtually absent among the AUEW group. Richter has noted that 16 out of its total of 17 MPs in 1966 had had experience as shop stewards or works convenors and Ellis and Johnson note that if one examines the pre- and post-1964 intake of AUEW MPs, the post-1964 members are significantly younger and none have formerly been paid officials of the union. [23]

In 1970 the NUGMW group in the House of Commons had only three former rank and file union members, the remaining nine being university graduates with middle class professional backgrounds. Their links with trade unionism and their own sponsoring union in particular seem tenuous. Nevertheless, they *are* sponsored members and they do include some of the leading members of the PLP. The other general union, the TGWU, appears to be hovering between these two strategies of adaptation to the post-war situation. Like the NUGMW it appears willing to sponsor members whose connections with trade unionism are slight or non-existent, at any rate until they acquire sponsored status. An analysis of the 1970 TGWU group comparing the occupational and educational background of those recruited before and after 1964 suggests that the NUGMW strategy has predominated in the latter period:

> Seven of the pre-1964 group are of working class background . . . the other three are university educated and of middle class background. . . . The pattern is exactly reversed in the post-1964 group . . . seven are university educated . . . three of white collar background. None of the post-1964 group are ex-officials. [24]

This analysis raises the question of how far the differences in strategy for selecting candidates for sponsorship may be related to differences in the perceived role of sponsored MPs. William Muller has argued that, historically speaking, the unions have not been very clear about what they expected from their sponsored members. [25] One might look for clues to the AUEW which appears to have adopted a parliamentary strategy just at the time when, because of the doors being opened by ministers and civil servants, one would have expected a growing scepticism about parliamentary representation. The principal study of the union's political orientations argues that its political commitment has to be seen partly in instrumental and partly in symbolic terms. [26] Instrumentally, the leadership of the union in the latter years of the first post-war Labour government came to favour 'consolidation', a term associated with Herbert Morrison and the majority of the Labour Cabinet. The union leadership was fearful of the possibility of a new leader of the Party bringing about further economic and political changes which they did not want. What they did want was to be free to bargain collectively in the context of full employment and the mixed economy as it had been redrawn by the post-war Labour administration and as Morrison and most of his cabinet colleagues wished to maintain it. Richter also suggests that the union leadership was attracted by the possibility of utilising parliamentary representation to protect its own position against criticism within the union. [27] The symbolic rationale of sponsorship revolved around the idea that although the union was industrially strong it was politically weak. [28] A further reason for increasing sponsorship, namely to maintain a working class presence in the PLP, is similarly considered to be only of symbolic interest by Richter because he can discover little 'operative meaning' attached to these ideas. What he means by this is that he found little coherent policy attached to these ideas — in the case of the belief that there should continue to be a working class presence this was in no way related to an ideological programme to move the PLP in a particular direction; it was a view that those on both the 'right' and 'left' of the Party could, and did, subscribe to.

Muller, in an extended analysis of the 'phases of union parliamentary representation', [29] has outlined a model which does suggest that 'symbolic' representation can generally apply to trade union sponsorship in the post-1945 period. For him the rationale of union representation in Parliament is summed up thus: 'Union prestige, symbol of consultation, service to Party and Tradition'. [30] Few students of sponsorship have been able to discern much serious use by the unions of their MPs for the pursuit of either major industrial or political objectives. The emphasis on the symbolic aspect may lead us to overlook the fact that sponsored members can be, and are, used for the pursuit of individual case work on behalf of the unions' members; [31] but this will be very similar to the 'surgery' work that most modern MPs undertake, allowing for the special interests of trade unions. Barker and Rush point out that this concentration on routine matters of individual case work appears to suit all the parties to the arrangement. [32] Minor concessions can often be made as a result of the individual action of sponsored members and this satisfies the union, the sponsored MP and the government for different but complementary reasons. It also suits the Party Whips whose interest is in maintaining discipline within the Party and who would be embarrassed if an external agent such as a trade union regularly attempted to persuade Labour members to vote in ways that conflicted with party discipline. Trade union MPs are aware of the doctrine of parliamentary privilege [33] which would appear to suggest that there are considerable limits to any attempt by outside bodies to instruct MPs on how they should vote or to bring slightly less explicit pressures to bear by suggesting to a sponsored member that his sponsorship will be reviewed before the next election in the light of his voting record.

An interesting case and one that throws some light on this past possibility is the behaviour of the TGWU in the 1967−70 period. At the union's 1967 Biennial Conference a resolution was passed which called for a reconstitution of the union's parliamentary panel. The debate on this resolution made it clear that the resolution's target was those sponsored TGWU members who had supported the government's incomes policy which the union had officially opposed. The 1969 Conference re-affirmed this resolution and the panel was duly reconstituted, omitting four MPs who had sat as sponsored members in the 1966−70 Parliament. However, it was not clear that the four who were dropped were treated in that way because of policy deviation − one, in fact, was an explicit opponent of the incomes policy. What is clear is that, both in the defence dispute of 1960−61 and in relation to incomes policy, trade union sponsored members responded to the demands of the Party Whips rather than the policy positions of their own unions. In 1966 80 per cent of sponsored members who came from a union which supported the government's policy at that time supported the government in the lobbies − leaving the remaining 20 per cent in a critical position. Of those union sponsored members whose unions did not support the government, only 35 per cent opted to act in line with their union, which involved repudiating the government and the Party's position to some degree. Very nearly two thirds chose to follow the Party line and *not* the position the union was espousing. [34] It is hardly surprising in the light of this record that some rank and file trade unionists in unions opposed to the government's policy should ask themselves what the rationale of sponsorship was supposed to be. The official leadership of the unions discouraged any condemnatory resolution at union conference, aware of the implications in terms of 'privilege' and probably more aware than the membership that the principal service sponsored MPs could render the union did not lie in the major areas of policy. [35] Similarly, most of the MPs who found themselves on the receiving end of criticism reacted unfavourably, not only because their views were being challenged, but also because they did not consider that the unions, as an external body, had any right to criticise their actions in the House of Commons.

Another way to examine the rationale of trade union sponsorship is to focus on those unions who have either strengthened or initiated sponsorship in the last ten years or so. NUPE has been earlier identified as an example of the former. It appears to fall into something of the same category as the AUEW: as the union grew during the post-war years [36] and came to play a more substantial role within the TUC and the Labour Party, it felt it should follow the behaviour of other major manual unions and sponsor a body of MPs. The fact that the union had serving as MPs one or two of its members who had been adopted as ordinary CLP financed candidates made the strategy fairly easy to implement. A formal parliamentary panel system was adopted in 1965 which enables union members to apply for consideration as sponsored candidates, their inclusion being dependent on a series of tests and an interview. The form of contact maintained with the sponsored MPs is also similar to that of many other unions. The MPs are asked to pursue individual cases and two or three times a year there is a meeting with the General Secretary and the Research Officer to discuss wider aspects of the union's policies. The union has been sufficiently satisfied with its experience of sponsorship to contemplate extending the scope of the arrangements for future general elections. [37]

The motivation of the three white-collar unions previously identified as having a growing interest in sponsorship is not altogether clear. Richter argues strongly that the major preoccupation of ASTMS during the 1960s was to build up its industrial strength, and its interest in politics was directed very much to this end. This represents rather a reversal of the sequence of events that was observed as occurring in the case of the AUEW where political expression was sought to confirm the greatly increased industrial strength of the union. [38] DATA (now TASS) certainly had no illusions about its parliamentary representatives. In advising its members on the techniques of lobbying it declared that

It was not a belief that the House of Commons can solve our problems which prompted the Executive Committee to produce a guide on lobbying. The knowledge that this activity is often carried out as part of wider campaigns prompted an examination with our MPs' advice on the way to achieve the best results. [39]

It was also DATA's Executive who provoked the resignation from the union of an MP who was a member, albeit not a sponsored one. This resignation was prompted by an Executive resolution which urged union members to examine the record of its sponsored MPs on the incomes policy issue. [40]

It is worth noting that one white-collar union, the ATTI, although much smaller than the three we have been discussing, has like them expanded rapidly during the 1960s and has discovered with the growth of the teachers' and lecturers' occupational group within the PLP that many of the new MPs are union members. This has led its General Secretary to discuss the possibility of the membership as a whole undertaking a more serious political involvement than simply maintaining links with those members who are now MPs. [41] The NUT, with which the ATTI has for many years had a close relationship, has itself sponsored MPs, though, unlike most of the unions we have so far discussed, these have been drawn from both the Labour *and* the Conservative Parties (and indeed the Liberals up to 1910). It has been concerned to maintain political 'balance', to establish itself as a group engaging in pressure activity solely in educational matters and to be credible to both the major parties. The bulk of the trade unions who sponsor Labour candidates only are well placed to exercise pressure within the Labour Party but so far as the Conservative Party are concerned they are bound by this strategy to be seen as a pledged group. One should note that over and above those specifically sponsored, many MPs will belong to trade unions (the bulk of them, of course, within the Labour Party). This is the current position of the ATTI which is considering moving to some form of closer association. The NUGMW, over and above its thirteen sponsored members, has an unofficial panel of MPs who hold a membership card and 'receive a small financial subsidy from the union for electoral purposes'. [42] Among this group are Harold Wilson, Anthony Crosland, James Callaghan and Elwyn Jones, Prime Minister and leading cabinet ministers respectively in the 1974 Labour administrations.

If, as appears to be the case, individual sponsored MPs are of no great significance, it may be asked whether the Trade Union Group which comprises all sponsored members has had any important role within the PLP. However, although they have comprised more than a third of the PLP in every Parliament, except that of 1945–50, there are a number of considerations which might lead one to doubt whether collectively sponsored members will be very much more significant than they are as individuals. In the first place, the PLP is sensitive about any 'party within a party' and, although factional groupings are endemic within the Party, any attempt to have a clearly organised grouping which aims to instruct its constituent members on how they should cast their votes meets with considerable hostility. [43] Although the Trade Union Group has 'a historic and special position within the framework of the PLP', [44] it is only open to sponsored members so that, however long-serving a record of union membership some Labour MPs may possess, they can only join the Group if they possess the vital qualification of sponsorship. This produces some striking anomalies, for instance, Douglas Houghton was for many years Secretary of the Inland Revenue Staff Federation, a TUC but not Labour Party affiliated union, and thus was never allowed to join. At the same time many Labour MPs *are* eligible for membership whose ties to the trade union movement are tenuous in the extreme. The Trade Union Group is also limited by the heterogeneity of the sponsoring unions and the clear differences in the political and industrial attitudes that they display.

The TUC does not devote much attention to the Group: Ellis and Johnson's comment that 'sponsored MPs overwhelmingly expressed a wish for closer liaison between the Group and the TUC' [45] is revealing, for there is little sign that the feeling is reciprocated by the General Council. Nor did leading ministers consider that it deserved serious attention: in 1969 Barbara Castle showed a preliminary draft of *In Place of Strife* to George Woodcock but was most unforthcoming with the Trade Union Group. [46] However, the Group was able to achieve a degree of unity and rather more influence when the proposals were made public. The evidence suggests that it was the potential defection of usually very loyal MPs in the PLP — many of them sponsored members — which led Bob Mellish as Chief Whip to warn the Cabinet that he could not guarantee the passage of the Industrial Relations Bill. This possibility, indeed near certainty, was crucial in forcing Harold Wilson and Barbara Castle to obtain the best voluntary agreement that they could with the TUC and thus abandoning the projected legislation.

There is no doubt that both the TUC and individual unions were active in opposing the Bill and the strength of this opposition must have been an important element in convincing many normally loyal backbenchers that, whatever their own view of the proposals, very grave damage would result for the Labour movement generally and the Labour Party in particular if the legislation was not abandoned. [47] But the likely refusal of support for the Bill's parliamentary enactment by a substantial number of Labour MPs should be seen as the key episode in the saga of *In Place of Strife* rather than in the opposition of the TUC. However misleading or ambiguous, Mr Wilson and Mrs Castle believed in the evidence of the opinion polls that the measures would be supported by the electorate and would thus earn them a handsome electoral dividend. Hence, however distressed the TUC might have been if an adequate parliamentary majority could have been assembled, there is no reason to doubt that the legislation would have been implemented. In the special circumstances created by the Conservative government's refusal to consult with the unions on their (the government's) proposals for altering the legal framework less than two years later, the Trade Union Group of the PLP did offer a focus for parliamentary opposition. This was taken limited advantage of by the TUC and by some individual unions, though not without some initial hesitation. [48]

### Trade unions, the Labour Party Conference and the National Executive Committee

The question that needs to be posed here is how far the trade unions can utilise the Annual Conference and the NEC to pursue their objectives either collectively as a trade union movement or in various alliances with the Constituency Labour Parties. Furthermore, it would be useful to be able to see whether any change can be identified in union strategy in recent years − is more or less attention now paid to these opportunities or is there no clear change to be discerned?

There is no doubt that the 1918 Constitution which has governed the operation of the Party with only minor amendments ever since does provide the trade unions with excellent structural opportunities to exercise influence both at the Annual Conference and on the NEC. The voting system used at the Conference recognises the force of numbers and trade union affiliations have always far outweighed those of the Constituency Labour Parties. Both union affiliation to the Party and CLP membership reached its peak in the 1950s − in 1956 for trade union affiliation and in 1952 for individual affiliation. Since then the figures for both the fluctuated by individual affiliation to the CLPs shows by far the most marked overall pattern of decline. The lowest point was reached in 1970 when the CLP figure showed a reduction of 33 per cent on the 1952 peak: there has been a slight recovery since then but the trend of declining membership seems clear. By contrast the lowest point that trade union affiliation has reached since its peak in 1956 shows a reduction of only some 8 per cent (this was in 1968). Thus, during the 1960s and 1970s, trade union voting strength came to play a more dominant role than in the two previous decades. [49] These changes in the relative strength of the CLPs and of the trade unions did not affect the NEC which only underwent one minor modification, namely the addition to its members of a representative of the Young Socialists. This brought the total composition to twenty-nine, eighteen of whose seats are normally regarded as being in the 'gift' of the trade unions. [50]

However, before one can make much of such figures other questions need to be considered. The most basic concerns the role of the Annual Conference and the NEC within the Labour Party. Most of the debate about this takes McKenzie's thesis as its starting point. [51] His historical examination of the Conservative and Labour Parties led him to doubt both the descriptions the Parties gave of their own distribution of power and the account they gave of their opponent's position. So far as the Labour Party was concerned, he considered the role of Conference and the NEC to be frequently exaggerated, not least by the leadership of the Party. [52] When the Labour Party had been in office McKenzie thought it impossible to dispute that the *locus* of effective power was with a Labour Cabinet and the Prime Minister, supported by the PLP. While he conceded that things appeared slightly different in opposition, McKenzie considered that this difference was a function of the relatively short period in office which the PLP had spent since its formation (only one period of majority power when McKenzie was originally developing his thesis). If the Party had enjoyed as long a period in office as the Conservative Party there would have been no question as to where power resided. [53]

One of the main criticisms of McKenzie's position directly involved the role of the trade unions within the party: as Henry Pelling put it '[the book] completely fails to comprehend the role of the trade union leadership within the Party'. [54] McKenzie has tended to resort to arguing that his critics rely on special or atypical periods of Labour Party history but equally one can turn the argument against him by suggesting that his thesis relies too heavily on the period between 1940 and 1954. It was the case during this period, as has been noted, that the Parliamentary leadership received the support of a number of major trade union leaders. This may have obscured 'the role of the trade union leadership within the Party' as Pelling puts it, or at any rate led to an unwarranted assumption that its character in the period 1940–54 was a fixed rather than a potentially changeable element. McKenzie has claimed that his analysis *does* take account of the role of the trade union leadership but the brief space devoted to it does suggest that McKenzie thought of it as being subordinate to the Parliamentary leadership (which may well have been the case between 1945–51 but is much more debatable in earlier periods), as well as not appreciating the consequences of a change in its political sympathies. [55] One might therefore justifiably conclude with S.C. Ghosh that any attempt to produce general statements about the distribution of power in political parties is too hazardous and that one should restrict one's attention to studying decision making in the context of specific issues or over narrow time ranges. [56]

The role of the Annual Party Conference certainly became an important issue in the internal affairs of the Party during the 1960s, due to the fact that some major unions and the Parliamentary leadership began to part company on some important aspects of policy. In 1960 Gaitskell's suggested amendment of Clause Four (committing the Party to common ownership of the means of production, distribution and exchange) was opposed by a number of major unions. The NEC, instead of making a fundamental change as Gaitskell and his allies wished, simply commended to Conference a twelve point statement as 'a valuable expression of the aims of the Labour Party in the second half of the twentieth century'. [57] In the same year Conference rejected the defence policy preferred by the NEC and the PLP and debated the role of Conference in policy making. So far as this latter debate was concerned, the unions did not choose to support the most radical motion put forward, which in the words of its proposer sought 'to bind our Parliamentary party hand and foot' to follow Conference decisions and the dictates of the CLPs. [58] One cannot find much evidence that the unions subsequently sought to pursue their aims by emphasising the importance which the 1918 Constitution appeared to give to the Annual Conference, although Harrison has claimed to find 'some sympathy with proposals to subordinate the PLP more effectively to the will of conference' in the late 1960s. [59]

Where one can discern a change of strategy by the unions in relation both to Conference and the NEC is in the policy areas that the unions have concerned themselves with. Both Harrison and Pickles [60] emphasise that it makes sense to think of the relationship between the trade unions and the Labour Party in terms of some kind of division of labour. Roughly speaking, this has meant that providing the PLP does not intrude into matters of industrial relations (except specifically to redress legal restrictions such as those imposed by the 1927 Trade Disputes Act) a good deal of latitude is permitted for the Parliamentary party in 'political' matters — particularly in foreign and colonial issues. Harrison's later essay notes how in response to the manifest 'invasion' of industrial relations by the 1964–70 Labour Government the unions lost many inhibitions about expressing their feelings on foreign policy issues. The most notable example of this is matters relating to the European Economic Community, but the defence disputes of 1959–61 established a good precedent.

39

It is important to note that the main thrust of union activity in policy making within the Labour Party after 1970 took place in the Liaison Committee and not through the customary machinery of the NEC and its sub-committees. The Liaison Committee was composed on the basis of equal representation from the PLP, the NEC, and the TUC. Each of the parties contributed its most senior personnel: for example, Wilson, Callaghan and Healey from the PLP; Jones, Scanlon and Feather from the TUC, and Benn, Castle and Mikardo from the NEC. [61] Additionally, the most senior professional staff at both Transport House and Congress House jointly serviced the Committee. The initiative so far as industrial relations was concerned was assumed by the TUC and by the middle of 1973 agreement had been reached on a procedure suggested by the General Council and subsequently endorsed by the Liaison Committee for three separate Bills. [62] This procedure reflected the TUC's desire to obtain the quickest possible repeal of the Industrial Relations Act. It was considered that if the extension of the rights of workers and unions which the TUC was anxious to see were included in an omnibus piece of legislation this would prolong the parliamentary progress of such a Bill. The TUC therefore felt that there should be three Bills: the first concentrating on a repeal of the 1971 Act, the second an Employment Protection Bill (extending trade union and individual workers' rights) and the third concerned with an extension of industrial democracy. Additionally, one of the first matters that had been agreed on by the Liaison Committee (again on the initiative of the TUC) was the establishment of a Conciliation and Arbitration Service financed by public funds but independent of the government. [63] (This had been foreshadowed by the voluntary scheme agreed on with the CBI in July 1972 and was particularly associated with Jack Jones. [64])

Two further agreed statements of policy appeared during 1973. The first was entitled *Economic Policy and the Cost of Living* and the second *Food Policy and the EEC.* [65] As early as May 1971 Harold Wilson had talked about the necessity for 'the right kind of social framework' as a concomitant of any prices and incomes policy. In referring to the possibility of a 'social compact' Wilson argued that such a policy would include action on key prices and a framework of social justice which implied the need for improved social services. [66] The emphasis on the need to control prices, especially the price of food, was an important trade union demand during the tripartite talks and in the judgement of some a commitment to food price control on the part of the Conservative government would have made an agreement on wages possible. The Conservatives were prepared to contemplate a form of price control, but only providing that this was matched by a corresponding form of wages control. [67] The TUC, of course, found this unacceptable but *Economic Policy and the Cost of Living* did represent precisely the arrangement the TUC were suggesting to the Conservatives.

After an introduction analysing the record of the Conservative government to date, statutory price control was offered as the major element in 'an alternative strategy':

> the key to any alternative strategy to fight inflation is direct statutory action on prices − and above all direct action on the prices of those items that loom largest in the budgets of work people such as food, housing and rents. [68]

After amplifying how a future Labour government would seek to control prices in those areas the other major emphases in the document were on the need for the redistribution of income and wealth, an increase in the state pension, investment, and industrial democracy. Having reiterated the previous Liaison Committee commitment to a repeal of the Industrial Relations Act and the restoration of collective bargaining, the only implied reference to wages was contained in the statement that 'They [the TUC, PLP, and NEC] believe that the approach set out in this statement . . . will further engender the strong feeling of mutual confidence which alone will make it possible to control inflation and achieve sustained growth in the standard of living'. [69] Though the document was commended to the 1973 TUC Congress by two leaders of major unions − Jack Jones and David Basnett − and favourably received by the Labour Party's Annual Conference a few weeks later, in neither case was there much substantive debate on it. However, Tom Jackson of the UPW and the then Shadow Employment Secretary, Reg Prentice, did suggest to Conference that the lack of specificity with regard to incomes was a potential source of trouble in the event of a future Labour government. [70]

The possibility of such a government came sooner than many at that Conference can have expected, hastened by the NUM's resistance to the Stage Three Incomes Policy in the winter months and their declaration of an official strike in February 1974. When Edward Heath called an election Wilson proclaimed that in place of the Conservative government's 'confrontation' the Labour Party could offer the 'social contract'. This would offer an alternative and peaceable method of conducting relations with the trade union movement. When the result of the election allowed the Labour Party to form a minority government renewed emphasis was placed on the contract. Labour ministers felt that they were justified in looking for a 'response' from the trade unions since a greal deal of their legislative and administrative programme in the first few months followed *Economic Policy and the Cost of Living* to the letter. However, it was clear that the major component in any such 'response' was a measure of wage restraint and many of the difficulties that had accompanied the attempt to devise acceptable voluntary policies some ten years before now came to the fore again.

In the first place it is interesting that Len Murray has consistently eschewed the use of terms like 'social contract' and 'compact': 'There's a lot of talk about a social contract. It's not a phrase I use: I prefer to think of it as an understanding between the unions and the government'. [71] The inhibition springs from an awareness that the possibilities of the TUC arriving at an agreed level or norm in relation to incomes, let alone satisfactorily enforcing the norm on its affiliates, are very limited. Utilising terms like 'contract' or 'compact' does imply a willingness and an ability to 'deliver' which past precedent gives little hope for. Within the enforced limitations of its workings however, the Economic Committee and subsequently the General Council of the TUC did succeed by the end of June in producing a series of negotiating 'guidelines' which were accepted by the Congress in September. Murray, as General Secretary, also undertook an extensive round of visits to the annual conferences of affiliated unions during the spring and summer of 1974 in order to try to build up support for the General Council's approach and to secure acceptance at the Annual Congress.

Nevertheless, the proceedings of these various conferences and the final debate at the TUC Congress in September indicated that behind the fairly general acceptance of the TUC guidelines and the idea of a 'social contract' there were wide variations in the interpretation of what these actually meant. However one might seek to sugar the pill with talk of 'incomes development' [72] it was clear that if the guidelines implied a measure of wage restraint they would not be supported in the actual bargaining situation by many unions. Equally, the old problem about how far a union had wider obligations either to the TUC or more vaguely to the trade union movement or to the Labour Party remained unresolved. This difficulty was raised not only by traditional manual unions in strong bargaining situations who would be likely to suffer from any voluntary restraint, but also by a number of mainly white-collar unions who felt that a social contract negotiated between the TUC and the Labour Party had less application to them. They did not possess the traditional ties to the Labour Party and therefore did not feel the importance of arriving at a better working relationship with it in order to repair the damages wrought between 1964 and 1970. Thus one had the somewhat ironic spectacle of members of the CPSA taking industrial action which threatened to slow down the pension increases which had been a key element in the demands made by the unions of a future Labour government and had been enshrined in *Economic Policy and the Cost of Living.*[73]

Despite these reservations of some white-collar unions what should be emphasised is that the principal vehicle for the articulation of the social contract and trade union demands of a future Labour government was the Liaison Committee, not the orthodox policy making apparatus of the Party (the NEC and its sub-committees). Obviously, the latter cannot be ignored, particularly with regard to policy areas in which the unions were less interested, but the establishment of the Liaison Committee owed less to the position of the unions in the structure and financing of the Labour Party and far more to the need of the PLP to negotiate with a major interest group whose co-operation it saw as essential for the success of a future Labour government. The historical link between the unions and the Party with all its force of tradition and sentiment certainly contributed to the assessment that the difficulties that had been encountered between 1964 and 1970 were not just the difficulties of a government and *a* major interest group, but of a government and *the* major interest group. [74] It was seen as especially damaging that relationships had deteriorated so far as in the controversy over *In Place of Strife* but this should not obscure the fact that any British government has to reckon with the trade union movement and has to work out what its posture will be. The significance of the Liaison Committee is that the policy of a future Labour government was being worked out by the PLP and the trade unions represented by the TUC, that is, the trade unions were an external interest negotiating with the PLP. Of course those trade unionists represented on the Liaison Committee such as Jack Jones, who affiliates one million members to the Party, also used the opportunities that were provided to reinforce the work of the Committee, but it was in the latter that their main thrust was centred.

## Trade union finance and the Labour Party

Martin Harrison's book produced the most detailed estimates of the Labour Party's financial position and the role of trade union finance in its overall structure. [75] Most people had been aware that trade union finance must be a major element in the Party's general financing but Harrison's calculations enabled it to be much more clearly specified. Overall, he calculated that seven out of every ten pounds the Party received centrally, and at least two out of every three it received for its regional funding, came from the unions. Given what has previously been said about the changing balance between constituency party and trade union affiliated membership one would expect those figures to have shown an even heavier dependence upon union contributions.

Despite one further major enquiry into the finance and structure of the Party under Bill Simpson [76] and the efforts of an unofficial pressure group [77] to revitalise the Party, little change is discernible in either its organisation or its financial situation. [78] In the latter there in fact was a distinct worsening of what had never been a very satisfactory state of affairs. After the trade unions had donated £91,000 in 1960 to eliminate a deficit on the General Fund which finances most of the Transport House expenditure, the first half of the 1960s proved somewhat deceptive in that the Party was able to more than balance income and expenditure, and thus to build up a new reserve on the Fund. From 1967, however, income failed to match expenditure and by 1969 the reserve built up after the 1960 deficit had been cleared was itself exhausted and the General Fund was in overall deficit. The Party had appointed Oliver Stutchbury as its financial adviser but he resigned in 1970 with the comment that 'financially and organisationally the Party is in a critically unhappy position'. [79] Although a rise in the trade union affiliation fee in January 1970 [80] provided some temporary relief the position had again deteriorated sufficiently for the NEC to appoint a special sub-committee on finance in 1971. This committee predicted on the basis of estimates presented to it that a deficit of £1 million would soon accumulate if no remedial action were taken and therefore recommended that an annual stepping up of the union affiliation fee would be necessary. The two previous increases had been in 1963 and 1970, but the recommendation meant that the increases would now be at an annual incremental rate of 2½p, so that from 7½p in 1970 it would double to 15p in 1974.

The Party had been able to meet some of its deficits by selling investments (in 1970 and 1973) and by a transfer from the by-election fund (in 1972) but it was quite clear that it was losing the battle against inflation so far as its own domestic budgeting was concerned. The contribution of the trade unions to the General Fund has exceeded 70 per cent in every year from 1962 to 1972, reaching a maximum of 78 per cent in 1970. The only new source of finance for the General Fund that the Party has been able to draw upon has been the weekly newspaper instituted in 1972 which has considerably expanded the share of income from publications. The Interim Report on Party Organisation which examined the financial state of the Party in 1968 made a number of recommendations which related to the role of trade union finance. Apart from the recommendation already noted that the affiliation fee should be increased the Report made certain observations about the nature of trade union affiliation to the Party. Six unions affiliating more than 250,000 members each accounted for more than 60 per cent of the total of trade union affiliations. Impressive though this may appear to be on the part of the major unions, the Report pointed out that the six unions collectively affiliated 850,000 *fewer* members to the Party than to the TUC. When one examined the gap between TUC and Labour Party affiliation for many of . the smaller unions the disparity was even more marked. Acknowledging that these disparities arose in part from the numbers who pay into the unions' political fund, the Report suggested that the Party should consider how far it could assist unions to enlarge the numbers electing to pay the political levy. It also wanted more effort to be put into persuading unions who did not affiliate to the Party on the total numbers of those paying the political levy to do so. The figures for trade union affiliation in the seven years that have elapsed since the Interim Report indicate little progress on any of these fronts. [81]

So far as other Party funds are concerned the other major one that relies very heavily upon trade union finance is the fund used to finance the Party's activities at general elections (there is a separate fund for by-elections). Harrison pointed out that the unions' reponse to Labour Party appeals for election funds tends to reflect the level of satisfaction the unions feel with the political and industrial situation in the period preceding the campaign. Thus in 1955, following a period of good industrial relations and general accord with the Conservative administration, the unions did not respond with much enthusiasm, in contrast to their behaviour preceding the 1959 Election when they contributed much more generously following a more abrasive industrial climate. This may appear a perfectly rational response on the part of the unions however much it may fail to match the objective need the Party has for money. Certainly in 1964 and 1966 they more than matched their 1959 response which is understandable in the light of the economic and political situation, whereas in 1970 their response was more muted. The total amount donated prior to the 1964 General Election was over £611,000, of which the unions gave £573,000 (i.e. some 94 per cent). [82] When the 1966 Election was announced the response was again considerable despite a favourable on-going balance in the General Election Fund after the bills for the 1964 campaign had been paid. [83] In 1970 although the sum donated was not inconsiderable — £513,035 [84] — it was given against a less favourable on-going balance in the Fund than when the appeal for funds for the 1964 Election had been launched. Furthermore, if one takes into account the decline in the value of money the 1970 donations do appear to signify a marked drop in the enthusiasm of the unions for the continuance of a Labour government.

Despite the apparent willingness of the unions to agree to the sharp escalation of affiliation fees in order to try to keep the General Fund solvent, it is by no means clear that this will succeed. Furthermore, inasmuch as it does, it will be at a level of organisation which has been widely agreed both inside and outside the Party to be hopelessly inadequate for a major political party attempting to grapple with the complexities of the contemporary world. It was against this background that the Queen's Speech following the February 1974 General Election announced that consideration would be given to increasing the amount of research assistance available to opposition front-bench spokesmen. This was supplemented by an announcement in July of the same year, to somewhat greater surprise than the statement in the Queen's Speech, that a committee would be appointed in the following autumn to consider the question of state financial aid for political parties. [85] The implications of giving even limited financial aid are considerable but the portents seem highly favourable for those who favour such a policy. All the major political parties are in acute financial difficulties and the 'argument from example', i.e. that many other similar countries provide financial assistance, is readily available. [86]

## The changing character of the trade union movement and of the Labour Party

In the final section of this chapter it is intended to discuss one or two issues that have been raised at other points but deserve a slightly more extended treatment. Both William Pickles and D.W. Rawson have noted the special kind of organic relationship which holds between the Labour Party and the trade unions and have emphasised how this may be vulnerable to social and economic change. [87] The kinds of change that are highlighted are similar, as are the possible consequences for the Party– union relationship, although Rawson qualifies the possibilities in the light of the comparative context he is working in. Changes in the class structure which were widely discussed by both politicians and academics in the early 1960s are one of the main themes they both emphasise. Pickles considers that there is a possibility of 'consumer consciousness' replacing

46

'producer consciousness' and that the trade unions are a handicap to any attempt by the Labour Party to take account of this, based as they are on an individual's role in the productive process. Similarly, Rawson reviews the argument about a reduction in class consciousness but feels that it is only at the extremes that the viability of Labour parties is threatened:

> A really class conscious proletariat would make life almost impossible for a Labour Party, as would a situation in which there was no working class consciousness at all. Between these extremes there is quite a broad span within which the extent of class consciousness will maintain a Labour Party. [88]

After the work of Goldthorpe et al. had confirmed the scepticism of many about the alleged effects of material prosperity on voting habits the debate on the relationship between social class and political allegiance has subsided. The major work of political sociology on the British electorate during the 1960s — Butler and Stokes' *Political Change in Britain* [89] — showed that on the basis of certain assumptions about the political socialisation process the Labour Party would actually inherit a *growing* constituency during the 1970s. However, they also demonstrated that the polarisation of the parties was perceived as narrowing so far as the youngest group of their sample was concerned and one could conclude from that a greater propensity to 'deviate' from inherited loyalties. [90] They were able to show how the swings in political support had increased markedly during the 1960s [91] and subsequent by-elections confirmed this pattern. Neither did the propensity to deviate show itself simply by increased swings between the Conservative and Labour Parties — the Liberals and subsequently the Nationalists ate into the former overwhelming share of the vote taken by the two major parties. [92] A preliminary analysis of the February 1974 General Election has pointed to the paradox of the result: 'while the traditional party allegiance to the social classes weakened, the Labour and Conservative Parties relied even more heavily on traditional class support.' [93] As many commentators and political opponents were not slow to point out, in both of the 1974 General Elections Labour governments resulted from a share of the poll smaller than any the Party had obtained since 1935. This, however, is unlikely to substantially concern the Party providing that their major opponent, the Conservative Party, remains similarly or worse affected (which was certainly the case in 1974). If there is any prospect of a workable alliance emerging among Labour's opponents, or if any further disintegration of Labour's vote is either registered or clearly in prospect which is *not* matched by a similar deterioration in Conservative strength then one can envisage a re-opening of the debate about the nature of Labour Party support. The analysis of Crewe et al. suggests that the Labour Party has been hit by middle class defection and it may be that the reactivation of the PLP trade union link between 1970 and 1974 deterred middle class supporters however much it may have helped to rally those among the Party's traditional supporters who have abstained in 1970.

The other major theme common to the discussion of Pickles and Rawson is a concern with certain discernible changes in the trade union movement and their implications for the relationship with the Labour Party. As Rawson puts it: '. . . a Labour Party is a Party to which trade unions belong. But suppose we ask which trade unions?'[94] He is making the point that a growing number of unions may not affiliate to the Labour Party in the future and the situation may become similar to that in some other countries where there are either rival federations which stress political non-alignment (e.g. TCO, the Swedish Salaried Employee's Central Organisation) or where there is a growing proportion of the work force that is not unionised at all. In Britain there was an attempt in the early 1960s[95] at an alternative federation largely embracing non-manual unions and it was also true, as Rawson notes, that the percentage of the unionised work force had declined between 1948 and 1964.[96] The attempted alternative to the TUC collapsed, particularly on the affiliation of its two main components — the NUT and NALGO — to the TUC and the deterioration in the percentage of the work force in trade unions was reversed between 1964 and 1970.[97]

But although the TUC was able to claim in the late 1960s to be more 'representative'[98] than at any previous time in its history, this is not similarly true of trade union affiliation to the Labour Party. Table 3.4 indicates trade union affiliation figures for the Labour Party and for the TUC, and expresses trade union affiliated membership of the Labour Party as a percentage of the TUC affiliated membership at different times in the last fifteen years.

The explanation for the drop from 70 to 55 per cent can be largely traced to changes in the occupational structure and the resultant consequences for trade union attitudes and behaviour. Non-manual occupations grew considerably and in the period 1964–70 the unions who organised in these areas were able to do more than simply keep pace with the increase in such jobs and actually increased their membership density.[99] This compensated for the considerable decrease in employment in such areas as railways, coal and textiles and the consequent reduction in the size of unions which organised such workers.[100] The difficulty for the Labour

## Table 3.4

### Affiliation to the Labour Party and the TUC, 1956–72

|  | Union members affiliated to the Labour Party | Union members affiliated to the TUC | Labour Party affiliates as percentage of TUC affiliates |
|---|---|---|---|
| 1956 | 5,658,249 | 8,263,731 | 70 |
| 1965 | 5,601,982 | 8,771,012 | 64 |
| 1972 | 5,425,327 | 9,894,881 | 55 |

N.B.   There may be a few unions which affiliate to the Labour Party but not to the TUC. However, none have been traced so far and the numbers involved would in any case be too small to distort the general trend of figures.

Party was that whereas the rail, coal and textile unions had been strong traditional supporters of the Party and had always affiliated a substantial slice of their total membership, the non-manual unions were much more patchy in their allegiance. The two main ones — NALGO and the NUT — both had a long history of internal debate about whether to join the TUC and one of the recurrent problems was the political implications arising from such an affiliation. [101]   What worried many opponents of affiliation was the sacrifice of a non-partisan position which they thought must be preserved in associating with a body that was in turn generally regarded as sympathetic to the Labour Party. Although this kind of opposition was overcome sufficiently to allow for an affiliation to the TUC it seems most unlikely that it will allow for affiliation to the Labour Party. The six major exclusively non-manual unions affiliated to the TUC in 1974 — ASTMS, APEX, TSSA, NALGO, NUT and CPSA — have a combined membership of over 1½ million but the last three, accounting for nearly 1 million members, do not affiliate to the Labour Party. With the contemporary uncertainty about the possibilities of economic growth it is extremely difficult to make any accurate predictions about the future pattern of employment and hence membership implications for trade unions. Nevertheless, it seems unlikely that the general trends of the 1960s will be reversed, even if they are slowed down and this does suggest that the Labour Party will therefore continue to receive a declining share of total trade union membership in affiliation. This in turn seems likely to strengthen the kind of development that the Liaison Committee represents where the Labour Party relates to the trade union movement as an external interest group rather than as an integral element within its own structure.

A conclusion of this kind might also seem to follow from the work of some of those who have analysed the social and educational background of the PLP. Briefly, the argument would be that despite the Party's almost exclusively working class origins the PLP has become increasingly middle class. The main working class element within the PLP has been the Trade Union Group of sponsored candidates but recent recruitment practices of some of the manual unions plus a change in the balance between manual and non-manual in favour of the latter suggests that this group can no longer be relied upon to maintain a working class presence. Despite the growth of the non-manual unions the trade union movement, it is argued, is still overwhelmingly working class so that in the fairly near future we will have a middle class Labour Party and a working class trade union movement. It is considered that this situation will make relations between the two much more difficult.

In evaluating this argument it is, as so often, not the facts but the interpretation to be placed upon them that is at issue. Providing that we accept occupation as the criterion of social class it is undeniable that there has been a growing 'bourgeoisification' of the PLP. It has been estimated that in the 1918 PLP over 90 per cent of MPs had followed working class occupations prior to election; by 1970 this figure was 26 per cent. [102] But what those who point to such figures often want to *assume* is a relationship between ideological position and social class. Thus this change in the composition of the PLP is linked to changes in the socialist behaviour of the Party or, to put the matter more precisely, it is assumed that a change in the class composition of the PLP can explain the emasculation of the Party's socialist commitment.

While relationships can be established between social class and attitudes or values at the level of samples of the general population, it is a hazardous exercise when extended to special samples of the population such as Labour MPs. Guttsman, who would be likely to support much of the argument that has been outlined above, nonetheless demonstrates how the Bevanite revolt, as an expression of left wing views, drew on middle class rather than trade union and working class Labour MPs for support. [103] Other invesitgations into the relationship between political personnel and social background have also shown that much more care is needed than has often been displayed by social scientists in inferring views from social or occupational characteristics. [104]

The information we have on the social background of the contemporary PLP is based on the Nuffield College series of studies of General Elections since 1945. Though these have unquestionably been an important advance on previous information about MPs they are obviously limited in terms of time and resources in how penetrating they can be. The formula they have consistently adopted has been to classify parliamentary candidates according to their 'first or formative occupation'. Even this can be difficult to discover from some candidates and there are problems in deciding just what should count as the 'first or formative occupation'. What the formula does not tell us is the social and occupational background in which the candidate grew up — or at least it tells us this only very generally and imperfectly by examining the information about educational experience. One does not know, therefore, how many Labour candidates have experienced upward social mobility and how many downward. Some indirect information is provided by Hanby's exhaustive investigation into the membership of the NEC between 1900 and 1972. Over the whole period some 22 per cent were upwardly mobile but when one separates out particular time spans the mobility rate shows considerable variation and a definite upturn in the post-1945 period — 30 per cent between 1945 and 1951 and 32 per cent between 1951 and 1954. [105] These figures can be no more than suggestive since only just over half the NEC in these later periods has consisted of MPs and there is no means of knowing how typical they are of the PLP as a whole. We cannot be sure how we should weight the significance of upward mobility without a good deal of further investigation even if we could demonstrate that it is widespread in the contemporary PLP. But before making any simplistic connections between certain measures of educational and occupational background and political orientations we certainly need to refine our analysis and to pose some of the kinds of questions that have been suggested.

Whatever might be revealed by a more searching investigation of social background, it is by no means clear that the assumption of a de-radicalisation of the Labour Party which frequently underlies such enquiries can be validated. Panitch has argued convincingly that the dominant strain in the Party's ideology is an 'integrationist' one, that is, its ideas and behaviour assume the unity of society rather than its division into conflicting parts which are incapable of reconciliation. [106] What this means is that it is hard to make out a case for some kind of socialist 'Golden Age' when the Party united around a coherent social and political alternative to capitalism. There may have been more socialist rhetoric in the inter-war years but as we have previously remarked the two Labour governments (making all allowances for their minority status) were at best social democratic in orientation, at worst little different from the Conservative or Conservative-dominated coalitions they temporarily replaced. This is not to say that the Labour Party was entirely 'integrationist' – certainly some of its voters and supporters did believe it was a vehicle for the radical transformation of society – but the dominant strain in its ideology has not reflected this, still less its periods in office.

What the general direction of this discussion points to is a scepticism about some of the more dramatic scenarios that have been put forward about the changing character of the trade union movement and of the Labour Party. Obviously, if the vast majority of Labour MPs will soon be middle class, either by birth or through upward social mobility, and if they have been educated via grammar school and university this will mean that their experience will be different from that of the majority of trade unionists. This difference in life experience and life style may well make for the occasional different approach to central issues of political and industrial life. But one must always be wary of over-exaggerating the contrast with the pattern of the past. It is not yet clear that the sponsored group of MPs is *inevitably* going to become more and more middle class and one must, in the light of the analysis we have developed of the Trade Union Group, be equally cautious about how far its working class presence has made very much difference to the operations of the PLP. Other developments which have been identified, particularly the declining percentage of the trade union movement affiliated to the Labour Party, are likely to count for more in any changes in the relationship. That development is more likely to stimulate the kind of innovation represented by the Liaison Committee, and changes in the social composition of the PLP (and in the TUC through the growth of non-manual, non-affiliated unions) may give an added stimulus, but no more than that.

## Notes

[1] Henry Pelling: *The Origins of the Labour Party 1880–1900* (2nd edition, The Clarendon Press, Oxford 1965), p. 201. Chapter 10 provides an excellent discussion of the final developments that led to the formation of the LRC.

[2] William Pickles suggests that 'Their [i.e. the New Unions'] special needs gave an additional and probably decisive stimulus to belief in political action'. B.C. Roberts (ed.): *Industrial Relations, Contemporary Problems and Perspectives* (Methuen, revised edition, London 1968), p. 262.

[3] S.H. Beer, op.cit., p. 145.

[4] In 'Book Section' *Parliamentary Affairs,* vol. 19 (3), Summer 1966, p. 375.

[5] Quoted in V.L. Allen: *Trades Unions and Government* (Longman, London 1960), p. 220.

[6] For detailed documentation of the impact of this on the membership of the NEC see Victor Hanby: 'A Changing Labour Elite: The National Executive Committee of the Labour Party 1900–1972' in Ivor Crewe (ed.): *British Political Sociology Yearbook,* vol. 1 (Croom Helm, London 1974).

[7] Quoted in Allen, op.cit., p. 237, footnote 2.

[8] V.L. Allen: *The Sociology of Industrial Relations* (Longman, London 1970), p. 178.

[9] Henry Pelling: *A Short History of the Labour Party* (Macmillan, London 1961), chapter 5.

[10] Including coal which Beer (op.cit.) shows to have been an insistent demand of the Mineworkers' Union in the inter-war period.

[11] Full employment is probably the most important of these objectives but there were also various proposals deriving from the Beveridge report which the TUC had been closely involved in.

[12] Guttsman, op.cit., p. 243.

[13] Ibid., p. 242 for 1945–51 data; 1964, author's calculations.

[14] Although there is some evidence of discussions between the TUC and the Labour Party, concerning economic policies for a future Labour government, the form of words used by the Party's 1964 Manifesto suggests that all the key issues on incomes policy had still to be determined: '. . . a Labour government will enter into urgent consultations with the unions' and employers' organisations concerned'. Panitch's account also emphasises how the discussions that did take place were directed at 'securing agreement in principle' and shied away from details. See L.V. Panitch: 'The Labour Party and the Trade Unions: A Study of Incomes Policy since 1945 with special reference to 1964–70', unpublished PhD thesis, University of London 1973.

[15] This detailed the proposals for altering the legal framework governing the activities of trade unions.

[16] E.S. Heffer: *The Class Struggle in Parliament* (Gollancz, London 1973), p. 246.

[17] Martin Harrison, op.cit., chapter 6.

[18] This was due to the Labour Party winning a large number of safe Conservative seats for which the unions have always shied away from sponsoring candidates.

**19** Until 1974 USDAW was the only other union to have sponsored more than ten successful candidates in the post-1945 period and it achieved this only once in 1964. Its pattern of sponsorship reflects to quite an extent its overall membership which grew, though very slowly, between 1948 and 1960. Since then it has declined, though again only slowly.

**20** TASS was formerly DATA and the AESD before that. The most recent title will be used through this study but it should be noted that it is now formally part of the AUEW, although its parliamentary sponsorship was under way some time before the merger.

**21** Michael .Rush: *The Selection of Parliamentary Candidates* (Nelson, London 1969). Appendix C outlines the major variants. See also the discussion in Ellis and Johnson, op.cit., pp. 4–14.

**22** Rush, op.cit., p. 180 *et seq.* and Ellis and Johnson, op.cit., p. 2.

**23** Richter, op.cit., p. 58–9 and Ellis and Johnson, op.cit., p. 7.

**24** Ellis and Johnson, op.cit., p. 11. If they are using 'white-collar' in its usually understood sense to denote occupations that while not established middle class are equally not traditional manual jobs, the comparison between the two intakes is even more marked than they suggest.

**25** William Muller: 'Union–MP Conflict: An Overview' (*Parliamentary Affairs,* vol. 26 [3], Summer 1973).

**26** Richter, op.cit.,

**27** Ibid., chapter 3 and pp. 102 and 114.

**28** Richter quotes Fred Lee, one of the union's sponsored members, writing in the union's Journal in May 1946: 'the union has grown to the position of being the most powerful force in British industrial life. On the political front we are absurdly weak'. Richter, op.cit., p. 54.

**29** W.D. Muller: 'The Parliamentary Activity of Trade Union MPs 1959–64', unpublished PhD thesis, University of Florida 1966.

**30** Ibid., p. 12.

**31** Fred Lee claims that 'The number of cases referred to us by the Executive Council on which we have secured satisfaction for the union must run into many thousands'. AEU Journal, August 1970 reprinted in John Hughes and Harold Pollins (eds): *Trade Unions in Great Britain* (David and Charles, Newton Abbott 1973), p. 94.

**32** A. Barker and M. Rush: *The Member of Parliament and his Information* (George Allen and Unwin, London 1970).

**33** W.D. Muller (op.cit., 1973) on the basis of over thirty interviews with sponsored MPs in the summer of 1964 that: 'The idea that privilege can protect an MP from attempts by his union to coerce him is widely accepted among trade unionists in the House of Commons'.

[34] The figures are dervied from Muller (op.cit.) who says: 'the bulk of union sponsored MPs did not act in agreement with their sponsoring unions'. In fact, his data shows that they *did* do so because most unions supported the government's position at the time. What he almost certainly intended to say was that the bulk of sponsored MPs *from unions opposing the government* failed to act in accordance with their union's position and predominantly chose to support the government.

[35] Frank Cousins in 1960/61 on the defence dispute and again in 1967 on incomes policy discouraged attempts to sanction the union's MPs (Muller, op cit., pp. 345 and 351). Jack Jones also argued against some of the more radical proposals put forward at the 1969 Biennial Conference (Ellis and Johnson, op.cit., p. 26).

[36] As previously noted, the union tripled its membership between 1948 and 1973 and moved from being the twelfth to the fifth largest union in Britain.

[37] I am indebted to Mr Bernard Dix, Research Officer of NUPE for this information on the union's policy (November 1974).

[38] Richter, op.cit., chapter 10.

[39] From DATA Journal, quoted in Hughes and Pollins, op.cit.

[40] Muller, op.cit., 1973, p. 351.

[41] The possibility of establishing a political fund was one explicit suggestion. See *The Technical Journal,* June/July 1974.

[42] Ellis and Johnson, op.cit., p. 10.

[43] Douglas Houghton, a former Chairman of the PLP, has said '. . . nothing is more strongly resented in the PLP than groupings of any sort which tend to become a party within a party' (in 'Trade Union MPs in the British House of Commons' *The Parliamentarian* vol. 44 [4] ,October 1968).

[44] Ibid.

[45] Ellis and Johnson, op.cit., p. 20.

[46] See Eric Heffer: *The Class Struggle in Parliament* (Gollancz, London 1973), pp. 99 and 101–2.

[47] This interpretation rests on the accounts given in Heffer (op cit.) and in Peter Jenkins: *The Battle of Downing Street* (Charles Knight, London 1970). Panitch (op.cit., chapter 7) generally supports Jenkins' account, though with some differences of emphasis as to the role of the unions and the PLP.

[48] Heffer, op.cit., p. 205.

[49] All the above calculations are based on membership figures given in LPACR 1973, p. 67.

[50] The eighteen are the twelve seats in the Trade Union Section, the five in the Womens' Section and the Treasurership.

[51]  R.T. McKenzie: *British Political Parties* (Heinemann, London 1955).

[52]  The oft quoted statement by the late Lord Attlee is illustrative of this: '. . . the Labour Party Conference lays down the policy of the Party, and issues instructions which must be carried out by the Executive, the affiliated organisations, and its representatives in Parliament and on local authorities'. (C.R. Attlee: *The Labour Party in Perspective* [Gollancz, London 1937], p. 93.

[53]  See particularly McKenzie's conversation with S.H. Beer reprinted in 'Book Section' *Parliamentary Affairs* vol. 19 (3), Summer 1966.

[54]  Henry Pelling, op.cit., p. 123.

[55]  See the correspondence in the *New Statesman,* July 1961.

[56]  S.C. Ghosh: 'Decision making and Power in the British Conservative Party: A Case Study of the Indian Problem' (*Political Studies* vol. 13 [2], June 1965).

[57]  The full statement is reprinted in Stephen Haseler: *The Gaitskellites* (Macmillan, London 1969), pp. 266—8 and the book contains a detailed description of the episode.

[58]  Labour Party Annual Conference Report (LPACR), 1960, p. 162.

[59]  Harrison (1974), note 15, p. 84.

[60]  Harrison (1960) and Pickles, op.cit.

[61]  The full membership in addition to those mentioned was: Houghton, Mellish and Prentice (PLP); George Smith, Lord Cooper and Sir Sidney Green (TUC); Chalmers and Sir Harry Nicholas (NEC). Minor changes were made as a consequence of elections (e.g. Edward Short to the Deputy Leadership of the PLP) or retirement (Ron Hayward replaced Sir Harry Nicholas).

[62]  *TUC Report 1973,*pp. 106—7.

[63]  *TUC Report 1972,* p. 106.

[64]  Eric Jacobs: 'Jack Jones, Leader of the Labour Party' (*The Sunday Times,* 1 September 1974).

[65]  *TUC Report 1973,* pp. 312—16.

[66]  The quotations are from a discussion of Wilson's speech and its general approach in W. Simpson: *Labour, The Unions and the Party* (George Allen and Unwin, London 1973), p. 221.

[67]  *TUC Report 1973,* p. 276.

[68]  Ibid., p. 313. The whole document is reprinted on pp. 312—15.

[69]  Ibid., p. 315.

[70]  LPACR 1973, pp. 117 and 122. Jackson spoke in very similar terms at both the Labour Party and the TUC Conferences. At the TUC he said: 'The TUC and Labour Party pact is welcome but it cannot be regarded as the last word. There is not sufficient detail and the gaps which exist could

be the very areas where misunderstanding between the unions and the Party could develop in future' (*TUC Report 1973*, p. 521).

[71] Len Murray: 'First Things First for the Unions' (*The Technical Journal*, May/June 1974) p. 6. See also the report of his speech to the Annual Conference of the CPSA: 'Mr Murray told the Conference that he did not know what people meant by a 'social contract' or 'compact'. He could understand deals and agreements but not contracts signed with iron manacles. He conceded however that there had to be an understanding between the trade unions and the government of the day' (*The Guardian*, 17 May 1974). And in an interview for the house journal of the Institute of Directors he said of the social compact: 'I didn't invent the phrase, and I'm not keen on it' (*The Director*, June 1974, p. 356).

[72] Len Murray's phrase to the NUGMW Conference, reported in *The Guardian*, 5 June 1974.

[73] NALGO also had a dispute between February and August 1974 in which Len Murray attempted, unsuccessfully, to persuade them against taking certain forms of action.

[74] Anthony Wedgwood Benn in the autumn of 1971 said: 'The party when in power alienated the most important pressure group of all from it – the British trade union movement. We now need their energy and they now need our leadership if we are to succeed'. (Quoted in Margaret Stewart: *Protest or Power: A Study of the Labour Party* [George Allen and Unwin, London 1974] p. 97.)

[75] Harrison (1960), chapter 2.

[76] The NEC appointed a Committee of Enquiry in October 1966 and it produced an Interim Report which is reprinted in LPACR 1967 pp. 334–353 and a Final Report which was reprinted in LPACR 1968 pp. 363–380.

[77] The group – Plan for an Efficient Party – was spearheaded by Jim Northcott, a former employee of the Labour Party, and supported by a number of editors of socialist journals, for example, the *New Statesman, Tribune, Socialist Commentary*. For an illustration of the group's analysis and suggested reforms see 'Our Penny Farthing Machine' (*Socialist Commentary*, October 1965).

[78] This was very much the conclusion of a group of essays published by the Fabian Society in I. Bing (ed.): *The Labour Party: An Organisational Study* (Fabian Society, London 1971).

[79] Quoted in Margaret Stewart, op.cit., p. 51. Some indication of Stutchbury's views and experiences can be found in his contribution to Bing (op.cit.).

[80] The Interim Report on Party Organisation had drawn attention to

the unsatisfactory state of party finances in 1968 and made various recommendations for increasing cash flow, including an increase in the affiliation fee.

[81] Panitch produces some examples of unions where contracting out *increased* between 1966 and 1968 (op.cit., p. 259).

[82] The Interim Report on Party Organisation (LPACR 1967), p. 336.

[83] £357,085 was donated, 'the greater part coming from the trade unions' (ibid., p. 29).

[84] There is no official statement as to how much of this total sum the unions provided but there is no reason to think that they did not give by far the greater proportion as in previous elections.

[85] The announcement was made by Edward Short as Leader of the House of Commons (*Parliamentary Debates,* 5th Series, vol. 878, col. 32, 1974). It is worth noting that the House of Lords, which has often foreshadowed developments in the Commons, had a debate on the subject in May (*House of Lords Weekly Hansard,* no. 900, cols. 1020—47, 1974), and the main speakers for the Conservative, Liberal and Labour Parties showed considerable sympathy with the idea of state aid.

[86] See, for example, Colin Jones: 'Paying the Pipers to Play the Tune' (*Financial Times,* 3 August 1974).

[87] Pickles (op.cit.). D.W. Rawson: 'The Life Span of Labour Parties' (*Political Studies,* vol. 17 [3], October 1969).

[88] Rawson, op.cit., p. 331.

[89] See chapter 5, especially pp. 104—18.

[90] D.E. Butler and D.E. Stokes: *Political Change in Britain* (Macmillan, London 1969).

[91] Ibid., p. 121.

[92] David McKie and Chris Cook: *The Guardian/Quartet Election Guide* (Quartet Books, London 1974), pp. 151—63 and p. 171. A concise documentation of this process is provided here.

[93] I. Crewe, Bo Sarlvik and James Alt: 'The Why and How of the February Voting' (*New Society,* 12 September 1974).

[94] Rawson, op.cit., p. 332.

[95] There is some discussion of this in Coates, op.cit.

[96] This is documented in considerable detail by George SayersBain, op cit.,

[97] An article by George Sayers Bain and Robert Price documents the changes in this period: 'Union Growth and Employment Trends in the United Kingdom, 1964—70' (*British Journal of Industrial Relations,* vol. 10 [3], November 1972).

[98] 'Representative' is used here to mean that its affiliates embraced the majority of employees who were organised to some degree or another.

[99] 'Density' is the term normally used to measure the relationship between the numbers of any occupational group who are potential members and the numbers who have been successfully recruited by a trade union.

[100] The NUM had a membership of 610,000 in 1948 and 261,000 in 1973; the NUR's membership fell from 454,000 to 174,000 in the same period.

[101] For the debate within NALGO see D. Volker: 'NALGO's Affiliation to the TUC' (*British Journal of Industrial Relations,* vol. 4 [1], March 1966).

[102] The 1918 figure is from Guttsman, op cit., p. 237. The 1970 figure is from D.E. Butler and M. Pinto-Duschinsky: *The British General Election of 1970.*(Macmillan, London 1971), p. 303.

[103] Guttsman, op.cit., pp. 270–2.

[104] See L.J. Edinger and D.D. Searing: 'Social Background in Elite Analysis' (*American Political Science Review,* vol. 61 [2], June 1967).

[105] Hanby, op.cit.

[106] Leo Panitch: 'Ideology and Integration: The Case of the British Labour Party' (*Political Studies,* vol. 19 [2], June 1971).

# 4  Trade Unions and Government

The conventional wisdom about interest group politics in Britain is that for business, union and professional groups contact with government departments is a prime objective. In a parliamentary system such as Britain's, where one party normally has a majority over all others, power is effectively located in the political and administrative Executive rather than in Parliament. The majority of Bills which are introduced into Parliament by the political Executive will emerge with few important modifications as Acts. This enables considerable consultation to take place with interested parties before the legislation is introduced into Parliament and facilitates a smooth legislative passage, as many objections which might otherwise be raised will already have been taken into account. Additionally, it is customary with much modern legislation to present the main principles in the Bill that comes before Parliament and to leave matters of detail to be dealt with by a considerable armoury of delegated powers which the Bill gives to the appropriate minister. In some cases the resulting regulations − or statutory instruments, to give them their formal title − will come before Parliament but the scrutiny tends to be largely formal. The actual drafting of the regulations is done by the minister or, more likely, by his civil servants, very often in consultation with interested parties.[1] Both Beer and Finer have analysed in very similar terms the underlying realities that are responsible for this close relationship between government and groups, Beer using the concepts of advice, acquiescence and approval, Finer those of information, consent and administration of policy.[2] What both are highlighting is that in a situation where governments accept wide economic and social responsibilities in the form of what Beer calls the 'managed economy' and the 'welfare state', such governments cannot easily execute these responsibilities without the help of particular interest groups. The concepts of advice, acquiescence and approval are used by Beer to specify more precisely just what this 'help' consists of. Finer's contribution is important in emphasising the mutual interdependence of groups and government, for it would be a serious misunderstanding of the situation if one were to suggest that the

61

relationship between government and interest groups was one-sided, with the interest groups always dominant and the government always subservient. The trade unions have acknowledged the logic of these considerations and the TUC is now included in any list of the important interest groups which have close and continuous relations with government departments. The unions came to concentrate on the strategy of seeking influence with government after having tried various alternatives — working through Parliament and the Labour Party, and direct action in the form of strikes, demonstrations and the like. It was in the aftermath of the major example of the latter — the 1926 General Strike — that Walter Citrine and Ernest Bevin, the former General Secretary of the TUC, the latter General Secretary of the TGWU, formulated an alternative strategy for the unions. The 1928 TUC Congress considered three alternative strategies. Firstly, they could attempt to create a revolutionary situation and work for the overthrow of capitalism; secondly, they could fight for improvements within the existing order using market forces wherever they were favourable and leaving employers to defend *their* interests on a similar basis; and thirdly, (the General Council's preference) they could further their members' interests but also claim a *share* in the responsibility for industrial prosperity by participating in the control of industry. This last course of action was what the General Council claimed they had in mind in participating in the Mond—Turner talks which had opened in 1927. The pursuit of influence in Whitehall can be seen as a complement at the political level to what the Mond—Turner talks were directed towards at the industrial level. Citrine speaks of his conviction that 'the trade union movement must exert its influence in an ever-widening sphere' and states that he and Bevin '. . . were both more inclined to look upon the constructive or positive sides of trade unionism than on the traditional defensive and somewhat negative aspects'.[3]

The novelty of this approach should not, of course, be exaggerated. Deputations had been sent to government departments from the earliest days of the TUC,[4] and Churchill and Lloyd-George in the 1906—15 Liberal Government had consulted the TUC on the establishment of Labour Exchanges and the National Insurance scheme respectively. In both cases the TUC was also invited to take part in the administration of these schemes. Citrine's contribution was to recognise that while some measure of consultation did exist, this was both irregular and confined to 'labour questions' — a rather narrow range of issues which were thought to be the province of trade unionists. He wanted consultation in these areas to be regularised, automatic, 'as of right'. But more substantively he also wanted consultation extended beyond 'labour questions' to include major

62

questions of economic and social policy.[5] Thus the appointment of two TUC representatives to the Ottawa Conference in 1932 is seen from the vantage point of the 1960s to have been of considerable significance: 'The interpretation of which questions are of interest to work people has since then been fairly wide'.[6] However, though this may make sense in the light of the consultation the TUC has been offered since 1945, the TUC's own history indicates that the 1930s were largely unproductive so far as the objective of widening the area of consultation to include major areas of policy was concerned.[7]

But within the narrower area of 'labour questions', as the *History of the TUC* and other contemporary sources testify, steady if unspectacular progress was made. Consultation was offered on both of the main points identified earlier, in discussions preceding the introduction of legislation and in the framing of statutory instruments made possible by the parent legislation.[8] Again, in this respect the effect of Bevin's appointment as Minister of Labour in Churchill's Coalition Government may have been somewhat exaggerated. Representation on advisory committees had greatly increased under Chamberlain's war-time administration while the National Joint Advisory Council had been established in October 1939. The significance of Bevin's arrival did not lie in the fact that trade unions moved overnight from complete exclusion to full incorporation into government but rather in a change of *attitude* — trade unions were now given representation and consultation as of right on all matters where they requested it and not, as Bevin himself had complained in the early months of the war, 'as an act of patronage'[9] forced on a reluctant government who needed labour co-operation to pursue the war effort.

Since 1945 trade unions have had a wide representation on advisory committees, Royal Commissions, departmental committees and a variety of *ad hoc* agencies.[10] Occasional rebuffs are recorded but the manner in which they are reported to Congress indicates that these are the rare exceptions to the prevailing rule.[11] The argument is less likely to be about whether trade unions have representation and is more likely to focus on details, for example, how much representation trade unions should have in comparison with other interest groups.[12] Whether trade unions receive full satisfaction or not on this count, it is clear that they have been able to secure a high degree of control over which *particular* individuals should take up those places which are allotted to union representatives. Although the TUC is anxious to extend its control over salaried appointments in the public sector as part of its campaign for greater industrial democracy, the majority of advisory committees and allied work is non-salaried and the TUC has expressed its satisfaction with the present arrangements.[13]

Similarly, in fulfilment of Citrine's aim of widening consultations beyond 'labour questions', the TUC has gradually extended the scope of its relationships with government departments. The Department of Employment in its former guise as the Ministry of Labour was the TUC's initial point of contact with Whitehall and it still remains of central importance. But is has now been supplemented by the Department of Health and Social Security and the Department of Trade and Industry which deal with many areas of policy of interest to the TUC.

One further development should also be noted. This concerns the movement by trade unions — and indeed by employers' organisations — from an advisory and consultative to an executive role. Two bodies in particular are involved here — the Manpower Services Commission and the Health and Safety Commission. In both cases, trade union and employers' representatives predominate among the membership. Both bodies have been established to exercise functions that were previously the direct responsibility of civil servants. Although the two bodies remain ultimately the responsibility of the relevant ministers, the Commissions do represent a development of some significance in that the interest groups most directly affected by their work are now exercising the State's responsibilities on its behalf. This arrangement is not wholly without precedent, in that the unions and the employers *de facto* if not *de jure* administered various aspects of the war economy between 1939 and 1945, but nevertheless those arrangements were regarded as exceptional while the present ones are intended to be permanent.

Concerning the advisory and consultative relationship between unions and government — which is still the predominant one — two major difficulties have been identified as allegedly hindering the successful use of the Whitehall strategy by trade unions. First, V.L. Allen has suggested that, however impressive the representational rights which have been granted to trade unions, individual trade unionists cannot make effective use of their opportunities. [14] (Allen's reservations have been echoed in a more recent study by Irving Richter. [15] Secondly, in an extended study of the various attempts to arrive at an incomes policy since 1945, Dorfman suggests that the TUC lacks some of the crucial attributes that are essential for successful relations between government and major producer groups. [16] Each of these criticisms will be examined in turn below.

The gist of Allen's case is that the style and approach of advisory committees is set by those who have received advanced education and training and are able as a result to marshall detail and present logical arguments. Trade unionists who sit on these committees are not equipped in this way, he argues, and are further handicapped by having multiple

64

committee responsibilities. At best, therefore, they are likely to exercise a negative effect on committees by 'preventing decisions being taken which are inimical to the interests of trade unions more by being present than by argument'. [17] Allen admits that this general analysis is subject to individual variation since there is always 'a striking divergence in the quality of union leaders, in the composition of committees and in the subjects under discussion'. [18] As he also concedes, there is an absence of written evidence and the verbal evidence available is contradictory. It should also be added that his analysis is of trade unionists on advisory committees and, though this is an important indication of a group's legitimacy in Whitehall, it is only *one* aspect of the Whitehall relationship and it is far from clear that it is the most important.

While, as we have indicated, political scientists have agreed on the importance for many groups of the Whitehall relationship, they have not devoted much effort to specifying precisely *how* the relationship operates and whether it is possible to specify that some kinds of contact are more important than others. [19] Four main kinds of contact can be distinguished: (i) the advisory committee, departmental committee etc.; (ii) formal deputations to the department which talk either to the minister or to his senior civil servants; (iii) informal contact — again, this may take place either at the elected leadership or at the professional staff level, or indeed be a mixture of both; (iv) written communications. The TUC enjoys all these types of contact in the many areas of public policy with which it concerns itself. [20] The information we have about advisory committees, [21] inadequate though it undoubtedly is, has led Walkland to conclude that 'They [the advisory committees] are seldom brought to bear on subjects which are 'political' in the party sense'. [22] We should, of course, be cautious about equating importance with subjects that *are* 'political in the party sense' but it is fairly clear that many of the major concerns of trade unions are the daily bread and butter of politicians: indeed the gist of the argument in chapter 2 was that politicians had increasingly 'politicised' areas previously the province of trade unions and employers. Many of these concerns are discussed through channels other than (i) above. Thus any overall assessment of the effectiveness of the relationship between the unions and the Executive would have to take into account much more than just the work of the advisory committees. There are very difficult problems involved here, many of which are familiar from other studies of policy making, but three in particular are worth mentioning. First, although the TUC provides us with a great deal of information about its contacts with the Executive — both as regards the form and the substance of discussion — we lack comparable information about the representations of other interested parties. Second, almost inevitably most of the informal contacts are not recorded. Finally, there are the difficulties associated with relying upon the record, formal or informal, when one acknowledges the concept of 'anticipated reaction' or 'non-decision' which cannot be ignored in any satisfactory assessment.

It is outside the scope of this work to undertake the kind of extensive exercise that we are suggesting must be undertaken before we can arrive at a more satisfactory account of union/Executive relationships. But by way of making a start, we shall examine here the trades unions' approach to The National Economic Development Council and its associated Economic Development Committees. This was a major innovation in advisory machinery of the 1960s and it serves to illustrate a number of the general points that bear on the relationship between government and interests groups.

⊏⟩Before doing this, however, we should consider the other major difficulty which has been identified in the relationship between government and trade unions. This arises from Dorfman's examination of the attempt to conclude an agreement with the unions on an incomes policy in the post-1945 period. The conclusion that emerged from this study was that the TUC was unable to bring the unions into a fully effective relationship with the Executive because of certain inherent weaknesses within the TUC. Again, we shall need to examine the approach of the trade unions and the TUC to the issue of incomes policy in some detail, but it should be borne in mind that although the subject of incomes is of central importance to the unions, it is very far from being the only subject where government and unions come into contact. In these other areas the weakness of the TUC is less evident and less important, for in many areas of public policy the importance of the TUC's advice and approval may outweigh doubts the Executive may have as to how far the TUC's acquiescence can be taken as that of the trade union movement as a whole − one of the crucial difficulties in incomes policy. Furthermore, the very fact that successive governments needed to obtain union agreement on an incomes policy may have made them willing to make concessions in other areas, precisely in order to facilitate good relations with the unions and hopefully to engage their co-operation in an incomes policy. The 'social contract' developed during the Labour Party's period in opposition (1970−74), is an example of this, but it may only make explicit what has been implicit in policy making for much of the post-war period.

Finally, we must stress the limitations of this approach that emphasises the difficulties that face a successful trade union/Executive relationship, if the criteria of 'success' is how far the TUC has succeeded in persuading governments to implement TUC policy. If we accept the emphasis that Coates has argued for in interest group studies of focusing on the *behaviour* of groups through a study of their strategy and tactics, then this concern with how *successful* groups have been is only relevant to the extent that it enters into the calculations of the groups in question and those they seek to influence. Thus the external observer may well conclude that at best the trade unions have succeeded in preventing governments doing what they want, but the unions do not, judging it to be against their interests. But whether such a conclusion affects the manner in which unions *behave* depends upon establishing: (a) whether they agree with such an assessment and (b) what implications they draw from it for their future conduct. It would be quite possible for them to agree with the assessment but not to substantially alter their strategy and tactics as a consequence. It is worth noting in this connection that the TUC's own evidence to the Fulton Commission declared that there was a 'consensus' between city, business, quality papers, universities and civil servants by virtue of their common educational background: 'Theirs is a very different perspective from that of working people of Britain, and basic social attitudes are likewise different'. [23] However, since the General Council shares the perspectives of working people it 'often finds that discussions with government on questions affecting the interests of working people are unproductive'. [24]

This is an interesting statement, suggesting that the TUC felt itself to be operating in a hostile climate in which it was difficult to obtain much sympathy for or understanding of what trade unions were about. If this did represent a widely held perception in the trade union movement, then a defensive strategy may well have made a good deal of sense. It would have meant that the test for trade unionists of the utility of contacts with governments was couched much more in terms of what they have prevented governments doing to them rather than what trade union objectives they have persuaded governments to positively adopt.

It should be noted, though, that the Fulton evidence pre-dates the major campaigns against trade union reform and the miners' strikes of 1972 and 1974. Though the campaigns against trade union reform in 1969 and between 1970 and 1974 were defensive in nature, aimed at retaining the *status quo*, both the Labour and Conservative governments regarded the attempts to change the trade union legal framework as being of central importance. The unions, first in deflecting the Labour Party from its intended legislation and then in pursuing a sustained programme of non-cooperation with the Conservative legislation, demonstrated the strength of their veto power. This demonstration, plus the ability of the

NUM to obtain the wage settlements it, rather than the government, thought appropriate, has increased the self-confidence of trade unions in their relations with government. They would in many cases still support the analysis of the bias of feeling that the Fulton evidence asserts, but they feel much more confident in their ability to make their voice heard when pursuing their own objectives. Such an increase in self-confidence would make sense, given the anxiety of both the Conservative and Labour Parties to achieve an understanding with the unions, demonstrated in the case of the former by the tripartite talks and in the case of the latter by the social contract discussed in the previous chapter.

### The trade unions and the NEDC

There are two main reasons for choosing to examine the relationship between the NEDC and the trade unions in some detail. Firstly, the NEDC has many parallels with the complex network of Whitehall committees on which, as we have noted, the trade unions have been widely represented since 1939. However, unlike many of the committees on which trade unionists serve, the NEDC was established with considerable publicity and its proceedings have continued to attract attention. Our first aim is therefore to study the approach of the trade unions both to the establishment of the Council and to its continued operation.

First, however, a word of caution. One should be careful in generalising about trade union attitudes to advisory machinery on the basis of an examination of the NEDC, not only because it is only *one* of a large number of advisory bodies but also because there are certain special features which distinguish it from many ostensibly similar bodies. Certainly when it was instituted, and at some points in its subsequent history, there were indications that one or other of the parties represented on it wished it to develop into something more than a further addition to the Whitehall advisory machinery. One clear example of this was the trade union insistence on using the framework of the NEDC for the tripartite talks with the Conservative government in 1972. These talks raise a number of important general questions about the relationship between groups (whether trade unions or others) and the government, and the compatibility of different kinds of representation in Britain. Thus the second main aim of this discussion of the NEDC is to try to illuminate in what respects it can be thought of as different from other advisory bodies and the various important issues that this raises.

The origins of the NEDC are fairly well known and documented. [25]

Faced with a deteriorating economic situation in the middle of 1961 the Conservative Chancellor of the Exchequer, Selwyn Lloyd, introduced the most emphatic 'stop' in the post-war cycle of 'stop-go' in July of that year. Understandably, the elements that attracted greatest publicity and most controversy were the measures to restrict credit and to institute a six-month 'pay pause' with particular emphasis on the public sector. Even those who agreed on the need to restrain wage increases were somewhat critical of a strategy that had included surtax concessions earlier in the year and made no attempt whatever to involve the TUC before announcing the pay pause. It is most unlikely that the TUC and the government would have been able to arrive at a mutually satisfactory agreement, but there is little doubt that if some degree of consultation had taken place the Chancellor would have had less trouble gaining the co-operation of the TUC in establishing the planning agency which was to become the NEDC.

The idea of a planning body was put forward in Lloyd's emergency measures but as it was it took six months before the TUC agreed to participate in the organisation and then only with an explicit disclaimer as to the government's incomes policy. An important part of the reason why eventual agreement was so long coming was the suspicion that Lloyd had engendered by his lack of consultation with the TUC over the announcement of the pay pause, allied to the tactics the government used in subsequent months to try to enforce it in the public sector. Although the TUC had little success in influencing the government in its implementation of the pay pause,[26] they did succeed in achieving a structure for the NEDC which they felt to be very satisfactory: George Woodcock was thus able to report to the 1962 Congress that '. . . we have got, probably because of our pressure, pretty much the form we wanted'.[27]

Although there was a degree of ambiguity and uncertainty (which will be discussed in greater detail below), the original conception of the NEDC appears to have been as an institutional pressure group particularly focused on the objective of economic growth. The TUC appeared to be thinking primarily in these terms when it finally announced its agreement to join in January 1962. After emphasising that the government's conception of planning did not match that of the TUC it nevertheless concluded that 'they [TUC representatives] should put to a practical test the question whether participation would give them a genuine opportunity of influencing the government's policies in ways which would help trade unionists'.[28] The rationale seems clear — the NEDC included major government office-holders (it was initially chaired by the Chancellor, and the Minister of Labour and the President of the Board of Trade also attended); the TUC would attend on an equal basis with the employers' representatives and would thus be able to outline demands and develop a supporting strategy in the general context of a body concerned with economic growth, one of the TUC's consistent objectives. In some cases common ground might be found with the employers and this would increase the chances of influencing the government to take appropriate action. One of the perennial concerns of any pressure group is to influence governments *before* decisions are made, rather than being confronted with an outline of proposals to which the government is already committed. The NEDC was obviously attractive in these terms, given the assurance of Selwyn Lloyd that, although they were only advisory in nature, considerable weight would still be given to the discussions.

However difficult it was for the TUC General Council to eventually make up its mind to join the organisation, and whatever the success of the delaying tactics as a ploy in ending the pay pause, delegates to Annual Congress expressed further doubts and uncertainties when they came to debate the NEDC. The debates that illustrate this best took place in 1962 and 1963 — the former after some six months of TUC membership, the latter following the publication of the NEDC's first two major reports. [29]

For those who had experience of the NEDC and those who supported membership, the NEDC was a further opportunity to influence the government of the day and should be utilised to the full since it has always been a central objective of the TUC to expand its opportunities for influence. George Woodcock faithfully reflected the continuity of successive general secretaries from Walter Citrine onwards when he declared: 'All through my time in the TUC, the TUC has been trying as hard as it possibly can to have an influence upon government'. [30] Government was seen as the source of power in society and as open to persuasion, not through slogans and demonstrations but through carefully prepared factual argument and intelligent bargaining. All these assumptions were attacked from a variety of initial premises. Some wished to argue that any attempt to influence a Conservative government in a way that was advantageous to trade unionists was a 'mirage'. In some cases this was justified on the grounds that the Conservatives acted directly in the employers' interests; for others the Conservative Party was seen as at times inclined to act in ways not always in line with employers' interests but ultimately prevented because the employers, rather than any government, represented the real source of power in Britain. In either case, belief in the power of reason to win substantial concessions for trade unionists was not very great: 'No ruling class has abdicated because somebody has written a book saying that a better system of society would help them'. [31] What was

70

needed was a much more agressive strategy: Woodcock's assertion that 'We left Trafalgar Square' a long time ago was countered directly by a delegate who argued that what was wanted were 'more demonstrations in Trafalgar Square, more outdoor meetings and not far less'. [32]

Probably rather more representative of the views of Congress were those delegates who, though prepared to agree that not much could be extracted from a Conservative government, did have considerable faith in what a future Labour government would yield. Some of those who believed this were concerned that close association with the NEDC, in which leading Conservative ministers were participating, would inhibit criticism of a Conservative government and harm the Labour Party. But at least one voice was raised in 1963 to warn of any idea that wage restraint, while inappropriate under a Conservative government, would be any more appropriate under Labour. It was argued that such an idea would be harmful to the Labour Party's prospects of winning an election and in any case against the basic logic of trade unionism. This latter point is certainly an accurate prediction of many of the attitudes that were adopted when Labour did form a Government in October 1964.

There was a further strand in the argument which is worth identifying, again as something of a portent of future attitudes towards a Labour government. In 1962 three white-collar unions protested at the assumption that salvation for trade unionists could only be found by looking forward to a Labour government. As the discussion in chapter 3 indicated a consequence of the increase in white-collar affiliations to the TUC is that a growing proportion of the TUC is *not* affiliated to the Labour Party and thus does not feel the identity of interest that many in the 'traditional' unions do feel. Though this did not worry some of the leaders of 'traditional' unions it was probably one of the factors that prompted George Woodcock's oft-quoted desire not to allow too ready an identification of the TUC and the Labour Party.

We have discussed Allen's estimate of the limited role that trade union members play on advisory committees and there is indeed some evidence about the impact of the NEDC on their role. So far as the TUC itself is concerned the impact of the NEDC is judged to have been considerable: it involves '. . . a more detailed and quantitative assessment of economic development and trends than was necessary when the General Council was confined to general criticisms of government policy and to sporadic meetings with ministers. . .'. [33] In the debate at the 1963 Congress those General Council members who had been most closely involved in the first meetings of the NEDC were concerned to emphasise the necessity for elaborated programmes and detailed policy statements representing the trade union position. George Woodcock, obviously a pivotal figure in the working-out of such programmes and policies, made no bones about his rejection of the politics of 'slogans' (as indicated above) and stressed by contrast the importance of a 'practical working programme'. Similarly, Harry Douglass advised the delegates that the only way to get a higher standard of living was by 'using your brains' and that Trafalgar Square politics 'created emotion and nothing else'. [34] The General Council's representatives on the NEDC have both taken the initiative in presenting papers for discussion at the monthly meetings and have also responded to the invitation to submit papers on particular subjects. [35] Thus one can discern a certain shift in TUC tactics whereby its defensive and critical posture — defensive in the light of attacks on it and critical of policies seen as hostile — is supplemented by detailed alternative analyses of the economic situation and the formulation of an alternative programme designed to further trade union objectives. These developments were powerfully reinforced by the invitation of an annual Economic Review in 1967. (This is discussed further on pp. 89—91.)

While the General Council's commitment to the NEDC and the associated EDCs has not been seriously in doubt since its establishment, this has, as we have already seen, not been entirely true of all the affiliated unions. This is borne out by an examination of the response to the Economic Development Committees which were initially developed in 1963/64 and now number around twenty. They are composed on a similar tripartite basis to the main Council and their terms of reference dictate a concern primarily with the efficiency of individual industries or groups of industries. [36] The TUC played an important role in their establishment insofar as they argued that they could not commit themselves to the support of various proposals in the Council's first Report until they had consulted the representatives of the unions most closely involved and consequently suggested that 'planning commissions' should be instituted as a means of tackling this problem of communication. But this was not the only reason that such bodies had an attraction for the TUC. Although they had joined the NEDC as a 'planning' body they were not under the illusion that the Conservative government's concept of what 'planning' involved was the same as their own. The idea of planning commissions was seen by the TUC as a means of stiffening the planning element:

> So far the NEDC has not been engaged in anything more than an exercise in indicative forecasting but in the General Council's view, much more than this will be needed. The next stage must be to translate descriptive forecasts into overall targets of performance and

to establish specific targets for major industries and industrial sectors. The NEDC has already agreed that it is necessary to establish systematic consultative arrangements with the major industries. Planning at the industrial level will involve two activities. The first is obtaining information on a regular and systematic basis about developments in different sectors of economic activity. The second is taking action where necessary to bring into line industries or firms which are failing to meet the plan's requirement. [37]

It was also clear, not least to the employers, that the establishment of planning commissions would offer an opportunity to extract information about industries which could be used in the customary processes of collective bargaining. [38]

However, trade union support for planning commissions or EDCs suggests either that the TUC's expectations of what they could be assumed to accomplish were pitched too high or that these were not shared by individual unions. When the General Council came to review the operation of the Committees in 1971 it revealed that general trade union attendance was below that of management, though this was subject to wide variations (from 87 per cent in wool textiles to 20 per cent in hotels and catering). But although conceding that the performance of most EDCs had been 'disappointing' and that 'by their very nature and terms of reference' they were management-orientated, the General Council still believed that there was scope for pushing them more towards trade union interests and it 'did not believe an alternative forum . . . would emerge if the EDCs were wound up'. Though 'planning' was out of fashion in 1971 the General Council argued that there were still advantages to be gained from membership on the grounds of 'a voice in policy making and obtain[ing] more information . . . for union purposes'. [39]

It has already been indicated that although the NEDC and the EDCs can be seen as a further addition to the range of advisory machinery utilised by contemporary British governments, there has also been a desire that it should be something more than this. Harry Douglass declared in the initial period of discussions surrounding the establishment of the Council that '. . . we as a trade union movement are not interested in any advisory body which is divorced from the centre of power'. [40] The proposal to establish a body like the NEDC was also the subject of controversy within the Cabinet, which does not suggest that it was seen as just a routine supplement to the existing range of advisory machinery. [41] The composition of the Council when finally agreed on by the three parties further indicates it is unlike that of most other advisory bodies in that it includes major figures in industry, the unions and government. Nevertheless, the government, through the person of Selwyn Lloyd, never suggested that it would have any executive powers, only that any recommendations it made would be given very serious consideration by the government in its economic policy making. However, it quickly became obvious to observers that considerable problems attached to characterising the NEDC as, on the one hand, no more than another piece of advisory machinery and yet, on the other, trying to argue also that its proceedings were to be much more important and influential than those of many other similar bodies. If the government wished the NEDC to be taken as seriously as it was saying it did, then the Council would have to be seen as a new and significant addition to the machinery for determining economic policy. In this case it was far from clear how the administrative departments, particularly the Treasury, would fit into this new system. Furthermore, there were also likely to be difficult problems with regard to Parliament, which would be most suspicious of such new machinery on the grounds of its account-ability and representativeness. If, on the other hand, despite Lloyd's assurances the government used the Council more as a sounding board, taking notice only where it was convenient or, worse still, used it as no more than a top level persuasive forum to 'sell' to the unions and industry policies already determined elsewhere, then clearly neither would attach much importance to it.

Despite the fact that the TUC subsequently referred to the 1961–63 period of the NEDC's work as its 'most creative period', [42] it neverthelsss supported the re-organisation undertaken by the Labour government when it came to office in October 1964. [43] A prime purpose of this re-organisation was the resolution of the anomalous position of the NEDC by transferring the planning function to the newly created Department of Economic Affairs (DEA). This meant the transfer of some of the professional staff attached to the Council (the National Economic Development Office) and generally a somewhat diminished role for the Council itself. It continued to hold monthly meetings and Economic Development Committees were created to cover a large number of industrial sectors. Although the responsibility for preparing the Labour Government's National Plan lay with the DEA, it was intended that the NEDC should play a role in commenting on the Plan. Unfortunately it was no sooner published than it was overtaken by the economic crisis of July 1966 and the need to take short term remedial action made the long term projections contained in the Plan quite unrealistic.

Although the DEA, of which so much had been hoped, was eventually abolished, the NEDC continued unchanged and its existence was confirmed by the incoming Conservative government in July 1970.[44] Despite the desire of the TUC when the NEDC was originally being discussed not to get involved in another 'talking shop', it appears by this time to have been closer to this kind of role than to any other. However, the TUC had stated its conviction in 1965 that the NEDC 'was sufficiently representative of the various interests in the community to be able, whenever necessary, to define the national interest'[45] and it was therefore not surprising that the TUC insisted on using the machinery of the NEDC for the tripartite talks between government, unions and employers' representatives in 1972.[46] These talks followed the miners' strike earlier in the same year and the conviction of the government at that time was therefore that 'We [government and unions] must find a more sensible way of settling our differences'.[47]

The tripartite talks which took place between July and November ended in failure, the three parties being unable to agree on a mutually acceptable bargain. The word 'bargain' is chosen since this was certainly the view the TUC took of what it was engaged in. Largely because of this, a degree of unease was expressed during the course of the talks by those who felt that they represented a pronounced shift towards a 'corporatist' style in British politics. While many of those expressing unease would admit that much of the contact between interest groups and the government went far beyond simple consultation and frequently did amount to bargaining, it was still felt that this was compatible with a pluralist approach to politics and the ultimate supremacy of a government created through majority party support in Parliament. At least three kinds of anxiety were expressed about the implications of the tripartite talks; first, that 'bargaining' was taking place on major issues of economic and social policy, not just on the details of policies; second, that the role of Parliament was likely to be peripheral with the government reporting any successful agreement to it and MPs unable to do any more than register their reactions — with no hope that these would have any influence; and third, that not only was Parliament likely to be diminished but that tripartism implied that the three parties were *equal* partners to the discussions and thus that the right of the political Executive to stand over and above the various interest groups in the community was under challenge. Trade unionists also had their doubts about the talks but these were more related to the substance of the discussions and the fear of what commitments their representatives were entering into with a Conservative government and the employers.

In the event the government were not prepared to negotiate on certain matters which the TUC wanted to place on the agenda; these were declared to be 'essentially matters of government responsibility'. [48] This suggests that the government was not in fact prepared to accept tripartism if it meant that some central parts of its programme had to be placed on the agenda ready for substantial modification in order to secure a voluntary wages agreement with the unions. Thus some of the anxieties expressed during the summer and autumn of 1972 seem a little premature, though they certainly raise important issues of principle about the relations between government and interest groups. The compatibility of what Beer calls 'functional representation' and the representation through political parties to Parliament has perhaps been too easily assumed by political scientists and the tripartite talks have served, as did the miners' strike of 1974, to force recognition of some difficult issues in this area. [49] So far as the NEDC is concerned, the TUC has continued to attach importance to it as a centre for the discussion of major questions of economic policy. Similarly, the Conservative Party continues to believe that the NEDC can be used as a key area of contact between government, the employers, and the unions and sketched out proposals for elaborating its role and concentrating public attention upon it during the October 1974 General Election campaign. Due to the work of the TUC Labour Party Liaison Committee, the Labour Party had arrived at an understanding of its own in the form of the social contract by the time it formed a minority government in February 1974 and, although it has declared its support for NEDC, it is unlikely to want to use it as a forum in the same way as the Conservative Party.

### Incomes policy, trade unions and government

It has been suggested that incomes policy should also be the subject of an extended discussion in the context of examining the relationship between trade unions and government. In chapter 2 it was noted that the commitment to a full employment policy in the management of the economy has altered the market position of labour. It has greatly strengthened the need for the advice, acquiescence and approval of labour as one of the major producer groups. Because of the vulnerable state of the economy the co-operation of labour has been particularly sought in the field of incomes. It is therefore obvious that the subject of incomes will have been one of the major points of contact between trade unions and government. The main focus of this discussion will be to see in what ways government has sought to enlist the co-operation of labour in its attempts to arrive at a workable incomes policy and to examine how the trade unions have sought to respond to the various government initiatives. We have chosen to concentrate on the experience of the last fifteen years, for although there are attempts at incomes policy before this period no statutory limitation was attempted and it was not until the 1960s that the subject of incomes came to play such a central part in the strategies of government, be it Conservative or Labour.

Before this can be done it is necessary to say something about the historical context of wage bargaining in Britain and to briefly outline the main attempts to arrive at a viable incomes policy. Whatever the different emphases of those who analyse the rationale of trade unionism, very few would disagree that the negotiation of wage levels and conditions of work is of central importance. In all countries which have any semblance of a market economy employees have associated (admittedly with wide variations) in order to protect and increase their wages and salaries. In this respect the historical experience in Britain of the development and growth of trade unionism can be paralleled by very similar developments in a wide range of other countries. But what *has* been peculiar about the British experience has been the heavy emphasis placed upon the 'voluntary' approach. What this means is that the State has played a rather peripheral role in industrial relations, particularly as the provider of a comprehensive framework of 'labour law'. What has been emphasised, and certainly preferred by the unions, is bi-lateral regulation between trade unions and employers' associations. However it should also be emphasised that there has been an absence of effective centralisation on the part of the 'peak' organisations of labour and the employers – the TUC and the CBI. [50] The latter did not come into existence until 1965; previous to this there were three peak organisations and although at that time they found it possible to come together to form the CBI, this body's subsequent history has been far from untroubled. [51]

The TUC has, of course, been in existence very much longer but it would be hard to argue that it had a very powerful role for the first fifty years of its life. [52] Following the re-organisation in the aftermath of the First World War [53] it has had a more substantive existence but, as innumerable historians have indicated, it has 'lacked authority', that is, it has rarely been able to proceed at a faster pace than the majority of the affiliated unions have been willing to allow it. Furthermore, this majority view can be ignored by individual unions without much fear of any effective sanction. [54] So far as the determination of wages and salaries has been concerned, individual unions have wished to keep the negotiation of these very much to themselves.

Since the end of the Second World War the pattern of national

77

bargaining between employers and trade unions has undergone important modification. Largely as a result of full employment policies labour has been in short supply in many industries. This has led to a situation where employers at local or plant level bid against each other for scarce labour and the nationally negotiated pay rates simply form a base on which to build considerable additional amounts of money as a result of local agreements. [55] The implications of this change in the pattern of bargaining for the *locus* of authority in trade unions are by now fairly well known: the work place has become important, certainly in many cases more important than the local union branch; national negotiations still take place but the initiative, in the amount of money that is demanded and in the eventual acceptance or rejection of national negotiations, depends less on the inclinations of the national leadership and increasingly on the views taken in the work place.

One further historical point ought to be made. Despite the seriousness of the war situation, particularly in 1940 and 1941, there was no statutory control of wages at that time or for the remainder of the war. Trade unionists did accept considerable restrictions on their rights but the framework of 'free collective bargaining' was maintained. The appeal in the post-war years to trade unionists to co-operate in the face of repeated economic difficulties and resurrect the 'spirit of co-operation' of the war-time years is somewhat limited if the sacrifices being asked for include that of 'free collective bargaining' since *that* was not a part of what trade unionists had to forego during the war. However, John Corina has argued that the overall 'package' which did distinguish the war years − '. . . rationing, subsidies, physical controls, high profits taxation, productivity campaigns, compulsory saving and manipulation of the cost of living index . . . supplemented by moderation in union wage policies' − has 'inspired its [the TUC's] vision ever since', [56] and it is certainly true that in the various discussions that took place between the TUC and various governments in the 1960s and the 1970s repeated echoes of this war-time bargain were heard.

Prior to the 1960s the two main attempts at incomes policy took place during the period 1948−50 and in 1956. The 1948−50 period was relatively successful (see chapter 3) but the 1956 attempt was much less so. The Conservative government that came to power in 1951 had pursued labour policies designed to 'preserve industrial peace' [57] and to prove false the Labour Party's gloomy prognostications about industrial relations under a Conservative administration. This inclination, combined with the relative improvement in the British economy in the early 1950s and the personality of Walter Monckton as Minister of Labour, meant that the idea of a government incomes policy receded. However, the consequences of such policies were seen to be inflationary and with Monckton's replacement by Iain Macleod the atmosphere hardened [58] and some attempt at a more direct government role in wage bargaining was thought desirable. The first of a continuing series of agencies was established in 1957 with the Council on Productivity, Prices and Incomes. This was succeeded in 1961 by the 'pay pause' and by a National Incomes Commission (NIC) in the following year. When the Labour government replaced the Conservatives in 1964 a voluntary 'Joint statement of intent on Productivity, Prices and Incomes' was achieved within three months of taking office. The National Board for Prices and Incomes replaced the National Incomes Commission in 1965 as an adjunct to this voluntary policy. The voluntary basis for incomes policy soon appeared to the government to be insufficient and a Prices and Incomes Act was passed in 1966, a year which also saw a compulsory freeze on incomes in the wake of severe economic difficulties. These developments met growing opposition from trade unions and were an important reason for the Conservative Party declaring at the time of the 1970 General Election that it would return to a system of free collective bargaining. [59] This it attempted to do but just under two and a half years after having won the election it found itself introducing a statutory freeze which was succeeded by two phases of detailed statutory regulation of prices and incomes. A challenge to this policy culminated in a general election which ended the Conservative Party's period of office. It brought the return of a Labour government now committed, like its Conservative predecessor in 1970, to abstain from any statutory role in relation to incomes.

In considering how governments have sought to involve the trade union movement in attempts to regulate the level of wage settlements we are studying how governments have perceived the trade unions as a major interest group whose co-operation is highly desirable and highly valued. There seem to be three main threads that can be distinguished running through successive government's attempts at incomes policy over the last fifteen years. Firstly, there is a willingness to discuss what the possibilities are for an incomes policy with the TUC, both as regards the substance of the policy and the machinery to be used for its implementation. Secondly, there are conscious attempts to fashion an incomes policy that will meet professed union goals, for example, the emphasis upon improving the situation of the low paid. Thirdly, there is the wish to co-opt union representatives to any prices and incomes machinery that is established; even if this is not possible the attempt is still made to persuade the unions to submit evidence and abide by any rulings that are produced. It is important to emphasise that not all these three elements are present in *every* attempt that has been made to achieve a workable incomes policy. The mixture is varied but at least one of the elements is present in all the policies.

In some respects the Selwyn Lloyd 'pay pause' appears to come closest to an example of an imposed policy promulgated without any prior consultation. We have noted in the discussion of the NEDC what difficulties the policy, and particularly the factor of non-consultation, created for obtaining the agreement of the TUC to serve on it. Although Lloyd recognised that the pay pause would be unpopular he had, in fact, deliberately linked the proposal for a planning agency to his policy on wages in the hope that the proposal would tone down the resistance to pay curbs. The Chancellor was aware that the TUC would prefer almost any kind of planning exercise to an espousal of free market principles, and that the importance he attached to the new agency would be attractive to the TUC as a major new forum for the exercise of its influence. So although the pay pause was certainly not subject to prior discussion, far less agreement between government and unions, it does illustrate something of the second common feature identified above. When the Conservative came to establish the National Incomes Commission in 1962 this was preceded by talks between the TUC and the government, although the TUC did not find it possible to endorse the body as it was finally established. [60]

All the various attempts devising an incomes policy since 1962 have been preceded by lengthy discussions with the TUC. The particular format used has varied but not the willingness to engage in a dialogue. The NEDC was the venue for attempts in 1963/64 to sound out the possibilities of an incomes policy but, as previously indicated, when George Brown assumed office in October 1964 direct negotiations between the unions, the employers and the DEA led to the Declaration of Intent the following December. Although the TUC became increasingly unhappy as the successive stages of the Labour government's incomes policy unfolded, the government was always anxious to involve the unions and the continuing opportunity to influence the implementation of the government's incomes policy created a considerable dilemma for the General Council. This dilemma is well illustrated by the freeze on incomes which the government announced in July 1966. There had been little or no consultation on this and it posed a considerable problem for the TUC in deciding its reaction. The 'problem' arose because a straightforward attack on the freeze — what the TUC itself termed a policy of 'outright opposition' [61] — would have prejudiced the TUC's general relations with

80

government and forfeited the possibility of influencing its policy, particularly in the post-freeze phase. Nevertheless, many of the TUC's affiliates wanted such a condemnation of the government's policy.

When the 1970—74 Conservative administration moved towards an explicit incomes policy in the aftermath of the 1972 miners strike the NEDC format was again utilised and the resultant tripartite talks represented a lengthy and exhaustive set of discussions aimed at arriving at an acceptable incomes policy. Though the eventual resort to a freeze and the two stages of statutory policy which succeeded it were opposed by the unions, continuing efforts were made by the Conservative government to involve the unions in the detailed discussions about the form they would take. [62] The tripartite talks enabled the government to obtain a good indication of trade union demands and hence to judge to what extent these could be met without jeopardising the support of other groups who were necessarily involved, e.g. Conservative back-bench MPs.

In tracing the second main element in governments' responses to trade union demands when designing incomes policies, the experience with the National Incomes Commission is again a useful starting point. One of the main trade union objections to the NIC was its narrow emphasis on incomes to the apparent exclusion of prices, profits and dividends. The trade union objection to this was reflected in the Labour Party's emphasis that its incomes policy, unlike the Conservatives', would apply '. . . to all incomes: to profits, dividends and rents, as well as to wages and salaries'. [63] Furthermore, Labour also saw a revision of the tax system as 'an essential support to a fair national incomes policy' [64] and accordingly committed itself to tax capital gains and block various tax avoidance devices. The Labour government tried between 1964 and 1970 to honour these pledges both in its incomes policy and by means of appropriate budgetary measures in successive Finance Acts. The importance the unions had given to any incomes policy being set in the context of a planned programme of economic growth was also recognised in the attempt of George Brown and the DEA to work out a National Plan.

When the Conservatives returned to office in June 1970 and embarked on a search for an incomes policy in 1972, they were aware that, voluntary or statutory, it would have to meet more stringent conditions than their attempts of ten years before. Harold Macmillan had realised that the Conservatives' original conception of the pay pause as '. . . an appeal to the commonsense and patriotism of all concerned' was, to say the least, a somewhat over-simple approach to the complexities of incomes policy. [65] The tripartite talks in 1972 served to inform Macmillan's successors of what demands trade unionists were making in return for co-operation in an incomes policy. Although the mix of statutory control on prices and a voluntary approach to incomes was unacceptable to the Conservatives as a whole, the government nevertheless made clear efforts to meet some trade union objectives in its final policy. In particular the formulae for both Stage Two and Stage Three were designed to meet the professed TUC concern for the low paid — both through the inclusion of a flat rate element in the cash formula and in the fixing of a maximum ceiling for the cash increase any individual could receive. It was also true that the controls on prices and profit margins were the most stringent of any attempted since 1945 and were extremely unpopular among sections of the government's own parliamentary supporters and with the major employers' organisation. A policy of rapid economic growth was resurrected from the middle of 1972 and Edward Heath constantly reminded the TUC that this too reflected one of the major priorities of the General Council.

The commissioning of the Pay Board (one of the two main agencies established by the Conservative government to administer the statutory policy) to inquire into the feasibility of a relativities procedure further reflected an attempt to make the statutory policy more amenable. It was a recognition that among the costs of a statutory policy are rigidities and inequities which are difficult to justify and militate against other goals the government is attempting to pursue. [66] From the Conservative government's point of view it was unfortunate that the Pay Board published its report in the middle of the 1974 dispute with the NUM since the report advised against using the suggested procedures for settling a major industrial dispute. The government initially accepted this point of view although once the General Election had been announced the NUM's claim was referred to the Pay Board under the relativities procedure. This was interpreted by some as compromising the basis on which the election had been called. Whatever the truth of this claim, it is certainly arguable that if the government had been willing to endorse the use of the relativities machinery as soon as the report was published it might have found a means of avoiding an election.

The third main theme that has been distinguished is the desire to incorporate trade unionists into the machinery for operating the various policies. The clearest example of this is of course the agreement of governments that a voluntary incomes policy, particularly one that is operated through the TUC, is to be preferred to a statutory policy. Despite the difficulties of operating such arrangements (which the experience of the 1960s made very clear), the Labour government returned to this arrangement in 1974. The major reason for once again placing faith in the self-restraint of trade unionists articulated through the TUC was the opposition which the Conservatives' statutory policy had engendered. A voluntary policy has a variety of defects but it is much more likely to receive trade union support than a statutory policy. Furthermore, demonstrating the inadequacies of a voluntary policy may be regarded as an essential preliminary before introducing a statutory policy.

When the statutory policy has been introduced governments are anxious to maximise its acceptability by offering appointments to the agencies that are used for its implementation. Thus, when the National Board for Prices and Incomes was established, Bob Willis, a member of the General Council and a former Joint General Secretary of the National Graphical Association, was appointed to it. At the same time all General Council members were nominated to serve on a part-time panel for particular investigations undertaken by the Board. Subsequently Jim Mortimer, who had been a full-time union leader with the left-wing union, TASS, also joined and three other trade union officials served for varying periods on the Board. Similarly, the Conservative government in 1973 offered places on both the Pay Board and the Price Commission to trade union representatives, but in this case the hostility of the latter to Stage Two of the policy led them to decide against nominating anyone. [67] Such was the strength of feeling that not only were these opportunities to participate in the agencies foregone but documents and review procedures were also boycotted to ensure '[no] involvement which could be construed as co-operation in the counter-inflation legislation'. [68]

The main impression derived from examining the trade union response to this record of events is a clear lack of unity at almost every stage on what strategy and tactics to employ. While hardly any union or union leadership rules out an incomes policy *in principle*, in practice most of the policies that have been attempted have attracted a considerable amount of hostility, particularly where they assume a statutory form. For many trade unionists a bargain with a Conservative government is very difficult to accept. There is a belief that the Party is primarily concerned with restraint and furthermore that wages will always be subject to more stringent control than either prices of profits. A somewhat more radical school of opposition to any agreement with the Conservatives would argue that it is not just a matter of whether there would be 'equality of sacrifice' as between wages, prices and profits, but that trade unions are in business to *increase* the share of National Income going to wages.[69]

Rather more trade unionists are prepared to strike a bargain with a Labour government — again the more modest case for an incomes policy will tend to argue that, unlike the Conservatives, Labour *can* be relied on to ensure equality of sacrifice. The more radical school will hope that Labour will itself be committed to increasing the share of National Income going to incomes and hence go along with the idea that there should be 'a planned growth of wages'. The foregoing remarks are based on the idea of voluntary, not statutory, policies since trade unionists, even if they cannot agree on how to fight the measures, will tend to find a high degree of unity in opposing any statutory limitation on wages. The resistance to statutory policies is historically grounded. As has been pointed out, even in the war-time situation the framework of collective bargaining was maintained, but this established tradition needs to be related in turn to the basic rationale of trade unionism. If the trade unions are to be superseded by government or a government controlled agency in the fixing of wages then a very important part of their *raison d'être* is removed. It is revealing that trade union hostility to statutory control was less strong when the latter was most severe, that is, during the two freezes. The important point about both of these periods is that they were clearly temporary expedients — there was always the hope that at their expiration collective bargaining would be restored. In neither case was it restored as the trade unions wished it to be, and particularly under the Conservative government in 1973 there was a fear that some kind of more or less permanent replacement of collective bargaining was to take place.

The main response of the TUC itself to the Labour government's desire for an agreed incomes policy was participation in the talks that led up to the signing of the Declaration of Intent and the endorsement of the various initial White Papers which established such agencies as the National Board for Prices and Incomes. The TUC was able to summon a Conference of the Executives of Affiliated Unions in April 1965 and received majority backing for these actions. Two things were notable about this conference. Firstly the fact that it was felt necessary to summon the executives of affiliated unions together illustrates the sensitivity on this issue of incomes policy: the assent of the General Council itself could not be taken to be that of all the unions unless there had been this explicit opportunity for endorsement. Secondly, the General Council received the backing of a majority of the unions but not of the biggest single union in Britain, the TGWU. Frank Cousins, then the General Secretary, may have differed in some of his political attitudes from his predecessors, Ernest Bevin and Arthur Deakin, but he was in complete agreement with them in not allowing for any state role in collective bargaining. [70] His resistance became an organising point for many other unions in the following three years as the expectations that

84

many had had about Labour's redistributionist policies were disappointed and incomes policy came to be seen not as 'planned growth of wages' but as straightforward 'wage restraint'. [71]

When the Labour government proposed its first statutory interventions in the autumn of 1965 the General Council's response was to propose to the Annual Congress that the TUC itself should take on a voluntary 'vetting' role of its members' wage claims, the hope being that if the TUC could demonstrate its success the government would abandon its own statutory intentions. Although Congress approved the proposals, the opposition was substantial — 5,251,000 voting in favour and 3,312,000 voting against — and did not give great hope that the 'self-policing' role the TUC was proposing for itself would be very successful. Additionally, although the increase in the authority that the self-policing implied for the TUC could well be seen as considerable, various decisions — both of principle and detail — necessary to its effective working were far from clear. The significance of the 1965 Congress decision has to be seen very much as a choice between the lesser of two evils for most trade unionists. The government was threatening legislation and the TUC vetting scheme, undesirable though it was to many, appeared as the lesser evil. George Woodcock laid great stress on the seriousness of the government's intentions in making his case for the TUC's own scheme:

> We have to take it — there must be no doubt about this — the government at the moment firmly intends to legislate. That is a fact. It is the firm intention of the government. The General Council had to face that fact and Congress had better face that fact too. [72]

Those who were opposed to the assumption of such powers by the TUC did not have any clear strategy of opposition, partly because their reasons for opposition were not the same and partly because in its voluntary, and indeed in its subsequent statutory, form unions were able to circumvent the policy to a considerable extent. Since both these points are important it is worth developing them a little. There were a variety of grounds on which trade unions argued against the incomes policies of the Labour government and the co-operation initially offered by the TUC. For some, any form of restriction or restraint on their freedom to exploit their market position was a contradiction of what trade unionism was supposed to be about. If they were charged that a planned society had to include wage planning then they would challenge the assumption that the Labour government was seriously committed to socialist planning and as the government's period of office continued it was not difficult to mount a case of this kind. In the earlier history of the government a number of trade unionists felt under some sort of special obligation to the government — there was a readiness to co-operate with Labour as against the Conservatives which has been noted earlier. Thus in 1966 John Boyd of the AUEW sharply attacked the criticisms of certain white-collar unions by asking whether it was '. . . too much [to ask] of you to make a little contribution to solve our nation's problems under *our* Labour government'. However in the latter part of the government's period in office rather more were echoing the complaint of John Newton, made in the same debate, that the government displayed signs of 'cannibalistic tendencies'. [73]

The white-collar workers were a complicating element. They did not in most cases feel under any special obligation to co-operate with a Labour administration: in 1965 a delegate from the GLC Staff Association declared that his organisation 'stands aside from the purely party political content and is completely uninfluenced by considerations of this kind.' [74] They were also unhappy about the ability of the TUC's vetting committee to take account of the special problems (as many saw them) of white-collar workers. [75]

It has also been noted that whatever the difficulties of agreeing on an oppositional strategy, the need for such a strategy was lessened by the ease with which many unions circumvented both the TUC's vetting committee and the government's statutory policy. The TUC's own vetting scheme operated from October 1965 to July 1966, was suspended at the start of the freeze and reactivated towards its end in November 1966. It was superseded in February 1970 by a Collective Bargaining Committee with rather wider terms of reference — by this time the government had abandoned a *de facto* incomes policy. The TUC established a 21-man committee and adopted a fourfold classification for the claims submitted to it. Initially it did not make any provision for endorsing any claim; on the critical side the strongest action it could take was to request unions to appear before the Committee and explain their claims. Over the period the Committee was in existence it undertook a great deal of work and initially attracted a fair amount of support, judged by the willingness of affiliated unions to comply at the minimum level of notifying the TUC of claims being made. However, in later years this willingness to notify declined, [76] and it is unclear how far the Committee ever managed to convince unions that particular claims should be modified. Given that the whole exercise, particularly the attempt to convince unions to 'think again' which, in plain terms, must have meant to lower their demands, was an extremely delicate one and a new departure for the TUC, it is understandable that there is little reliable information available to judge its relative success or failure. It is clear, though, on the TUC's own admission, that a certain number of claims when originally submitted to the Committee did not satisfy the criteria it was working with, and whatever success the Committee had in persuading unions to modify them this was not sufficient in the eyes of the government. [77] As George Woodcock constantly emphasised, the government was looking for quick results which he believed to be quite unrealistic. He argued that since the exercise was such a radical departure one could not possibly hope for immediate success. He also took the view that, far from supplementing the voluntary system with legal reserve powers (which is what the Labour government claimed to be doing), the existence of such powers made the voluntary system more difficult to work. Perhaps the major justification for the TUC continuing with its own wage vetting machinery once the government had introduced legal reserve powers was to provide itself with the information to intervene on behalf of unions when the Department of Employment raised objections to a wage claim. [78] This meant that even though the TUC had lost the battle to ward off the government's intervention in wage bargaining it could at least offer to its affiliates the possibility of ameliorating the impact of the legal powers in particular cases. It was considerations of this kind that led the General Council to its reluctant acquiescence in the July 1966 freeze. When considering its attitude towards this it considered four alternative courses of action varying from support for the freeze and co-operation in its implementation to 'outright opposition'. The various courses of action involving hostility were rejected partly because of fears about the consequences (e.g. an adverse effect on sterling and increased unemployment) and partly because of the consequences for the 'relations between government and the trade union movement, given the expressed determination of government to carry the policy through'. [79] This latter phrase acknowledges that a freeze was going to be implemented by the government and the main result of TUC opposition (apart from the aforementioned effect on sterling and employment) would have been to put it in a position of impotence *vis à vis* the manner in which the freeze was implemented. Similarly, in the following year, when the reserve powers were operating and indeed when the DEA was considering *extending* their application, although the TUC was angry about this a lot of its actual discussions were directed at obtaining closer TUC involvement in the administration of the reserve powers. [80]

Despite the opposition of trade unions to the operation of the reserve powers and the series of wage 'norms' adumbrated in successive White Papers, many trade unionists succeeded in achieving rises above the government-desired norm. A major reason for this is the bargaining situation earlier described as increasingly characteristic of industry in Britain. While some attempts were made to confine national agreements to the government norms, the additions obtained through factory and plant bargaining enabled many workers to obtain further increases. Professor Turner has pointed out that not only did the incomes policy not succeed in confronting this problem, but that ironically the official blessing given to productivity deals also provided a further independent stimulus to the growth of plant bargaining. [81] This type of bargaining was not available to all trade unionists and thus overall opposition to the policy rather than evasion tactics had to be the strategy followed by such unions. Resistance to the policy judged by resolutions at Annual Congress increased so that by 1969 sufficient support had accumulated for a root and branch opposition motion to incomes policy to muster a majority. [82]

It was not surprising, therefore, that when the Conservative government came to introduce its statutory policy in November 1972 it met strong hostility. Not only was the experience of the Labour government's policy still fresh in the minds of most trade unionists but there were also special difficulties in the relationship between the unions and the Conservative Party resulting from the passage of the Industrial Relations Act in 1971; it was observed earlier that many trade unionists find any incomes bargain with a Conservative government difficult to contemplate and on top of all these factors the character of the policy the Conservative government proposed for Stages Two and Three was especially irritating. Its limits on wage levels and scrutiny mechanisms were far more stringent than anything attempted by the previous Labour government. More than that, the legal powers assumed suggested to the General Council that the policy was not just designed to deal with immediate problems but that 'it also establishes[d] the framework for a *permanent system of statutory wage control'*. [83] Trade unions were therefore confronted with a policy very much more difficult to circumvent and with more threatening long term possibilities than either their own voluntary vetting arrangements or the Labour government's policy.

The need to devise an opposition strategy *as a trade union movement* was clearly greater and, it might also be argued, much easier for there were no complicating ties of loyalty as there had been with the Labour government. Up to a point the record shows this to be the case but the debate that took place at the Special Congress, called to formulate an opposition strategy, indicates that beyond a united dislike of what the Conservative government was proposing it was still difficult to advance. The recommendations the General Council felt able to make indicated this and although these were strengthened by the adoption of a motion 'inviting' affiliated unions to participate in a one day stoppage, the terminology, as so often, is revealing. The actual response to this invitation some two months later, further indicated the difficulties of acting as a united trade union movement. (This is discussed further in chapter 5.)

One of the main aims of this discussion of trade union response to prices and incomes policy has been to cast some light on the relationship between the TUC and its affiliates and to emphasise the difficulties involved in arriving at an agreed common strategy. It has been suggested earlier that prices and incomes policies have also affected the working methods of the TUC. These changes further illuminate the debate about how this relationship should be structured as well as telling us something about the views of the TUC on how to influence government. The major development directly stimulated by the prices and incomes policy was the series of TUC Economic Reviews which have now been published annually since 1967. Hughes and Pollins suggest that these Reviews have come to represent 'the main source of alternative economic analysis'. [84] In their consideration of the impact of the first three of the Reviews the General Council acknowledge the importance of the incomes policy as a stimulus to the TUC in developing its own criteria, given their refusal to endorse those of the government. Their disagreement with the then Labour government was wider, however, than one about the criteria appropriate for wage increases and they therefore wished to formulate a general alternative economic policy. [85]

The discussion of the formation of the NEDC indicated that those members of the General Council who had had the closest contact with government were the most impatient with the 'politics of slogans' and the most anxious to formulate detailed alternative plans representing the trade union position which could be put to government. The same emphasis recurs in the initiation of the Economic Review. Sir Sidney Greene, Chairman of the TUC's Economic Committee in 1968, complained that it was no use simply denouncing the government for having deviated from socialist goals. Aware that the critics of the government wanted the TUC to press 'socialist policies' on the government, he argued that 'we need to agree what the socialist policies are' and that the government itself was unreceptive to general denunciation and the proferring of generalised alternatives: 'you've got to tell them in pretty detailed terms what the alternative is'. [86] George Woodcock similarly recommended the Economic Review in terms very redolent of his endorsement of the NEDC some five years previously: 'We do not lack opportunities these days . . . what we need now is to improve our capacity to use these opportunities, to match with our wits what we have already got in the form of physical opportunities'. [87]

The Economic Review represents the TUC's attempt at an alternative in 'pretty detailed terms'. Although detailed policy statements had been produced before on particular matters, nothing comparable to an annual economic statement had been attempted. Furthermore, the TUC has made a serious effort to mobilise support behind successive Reviews by holding conferences of the executives of all the affiliated unions, shortly after the Reviews are published. The timing of the publication of the Reviews — normally in February — was intended to maximise their impact so far as bringing pressure to bear on the Chancellor of the Exchequer *vis-à-vis* his impending Budget was concerned. It was also hoped that it would be produced in time to influence the debates in union conferences held in the spring and early summer. Nevertheless, it was frequently the case that the Chancellor had already rejected some of the central claims made in the Reviews by the time the Conference of Union Executives took place and many unions came to the Conference with their minds already made up. Not surprisingly, the General Council felt that this gave the debates at the Conference 'a degree of unreality'. [88] The General Council also agreed on a procedure which allowed only for the complete acceptance or rejection of the Review and while this may have been intended to concentrate the delegates on the overall direction of the Review and not to give the appearance of considerable disunity, it undoubtedly caused resentment and may have lessened the commitment to it of some unions.

The General Council itself identified two main difficulties in its 1969 report: firstly, the failure of the Economic Reviews so far to influence the direction of the government's economic policy to any significant extent; secondly, the construction and presentation of the Reviews posed an awkward dilemma — in terms of their serving as documents to challenge the government they had to be lengthy and complex, but the more this was the case the more incomprehensible they became to the vast majority of trade unionists. [89] Various attempts were made to deal with this: in 1970 nine conferences were organised in different parts of the country to discuss the contents of that year's Review. They encompassed a total of 1850 delegates and the emphasis was on trade union officials and shop stewards, presumably on the basis that as 'opinion leaders' they could be relied upon to diffuse the broad content of the Review to a wider audience. However, the Annual Congress of the TUC has not paid much attention to the Reviews; in 1968 Tom Jackson complained that 'If a quarter of the energy devoted to destroying the TUC vetting machinery had been given to explanation and discussion of the TUC Economic

Review then this movement and this Conference would have been the better for it'.[90]

The TUC have nevertheless persisted with the Review despite seeing it ignored by governments and by many of its own affiliates. Since their introduction in 1967 the Annual Congress and the Conference of Executives have frequently found themselves reacting to government initiatives which they are opposed to and consequently the focus of both has been much more on trying to formulate an agreed defensive strategy rather than on formulating alternative policy goals.[91] Bill Kendall of the CPSA was probably rather more scathing than most when he declared at the Special Congress in 1973 that '. . . all we have on offer at the moment is a great economic thesis which will have of itself as much impact as a wet sponge' and would be ignored as 'all the others that have gone before it'[92] but the overall tone of the proceedings was on the action that the unions could take to defeat the statutory policies of the Conservative govern-ment, not on the niceties of what alternative economic policy the TUC should adopt. The main success achieved by the Reviews at this point in time seems not to be with governments but in the policy making of the Labour Party when it was in opposition between 1970 and 1974, and the major economic document produced by the Liaison Committee — *Economic Policy and the Cost of Living* — was jointly based on the 1972 Economic Review and the NEC's policy statement *Programme for Britain.*[93]

## Notes

[1] For a particularly illuminating discussion of this see S.A. Walkland: *The Legislative Process* (George Allen and Unwin, London 1968), chapter 4.

[2] S.H. Beer, op.cit., p. 310 *et seq.* S.E. Finer: *Anonymous Empire* (Pall Mall, London 1958), p. 30 *et seq.*

[3] Lord Citrine: *Men and Work* (Hutchinson, London 1964), pp. 238–9.

[4] For examples of such deputations in the nineteenth century see H.A. Clegg, Alan Fox and A.F. Thompson: *A History of British Trade Unions since 1889, Volume 1, 1889–1910* (Oxford University Press, London 1964), p. 252 and 264–5.

[5] Citrine, op.cit., p. 238.

[6] *Trade Unionism* (TUC, London 1966), p. 67.

[7] 'On major issues of trade and industry, poverty and unemployment, collective security and rearmament, peace and war, the TUC in the 1930s

found it almost impossible to get a serious hearing from the National Government, the Baldwin Government or the Chamberlain Government.' (L. Birch [ed.]: *The History of the TUC 1868–1968* [TUC, London 1968], p. 84.)

[8] Ibid. See also W. Milne Bailey: *Trade Unions and the State* (George Allen and Unwin, London 1934), pp. 145 and 364; and John Price: *Organised Labour in the War* (Penguin Books, Harmondsworth 1940), pp. 22 and 42–3.

[9] Bevin was writing in the TGWU *Record* (October 1939), quoted in Price, ibid.

[10] There are difficulties of definition but the number of advisory committees on which the TUC has representatives seems to have remained at around sixty for most of the post-war period, though this figure will disguise individual changes.

[11] In 1965 the Minister of Health accepted the case for an enquiry into drug pricing but did not appoint either of the TUC's nominees to the committee. The General Council argued that the minister was 'departing from customary practice' (*TUC Report 1965*, pp. 305–6).

[12] Interview with Mr John Monks, Assistant Secretary of the TUC's Organisation and Industrial Relations Department. Compare also Vic Feather's view that the Donovan Commission would have been a better body if it had consisted of four trade unionists and four employers (quoted in Heffer, op.cit., p. 98).

[13] *TUC Report 1973*, p. 401 and 417–8.

[14] V.L. Allen: *Trade Unions and the Government* (Longmans, London 1960), pp. 36–41.

[15] Irving Richter: *Political Purpose in Trade Unions* (George Allen and Unwin, London 1973), pp. 106–7.

[16] G.A. Dorfman: *Wage Politics in Britain 1945–1967* (Charles Knight, London 1974).

[17] Allen, op.cit., p. 40.

[18] Ibid, p. 37.

[19] Allen Potter's is one of the most detailed discussions of interest group/executive relations but it is more concerned to specify what the relationships are concerned with rather than the particular channels through which they are conducted. See A.M. Potter: *Organised Groups in British National Politics* (Faber and Faber, London 1961).

[20] See, for example, the TUC's evidence to the Donovan Commission and the Fulton Committee in Trade Unionism, op.cit., pp. 66–7 and the *TUC Report 1967*, p. 380 *et seq.*, as well as George Woodcock's comments quoted in Tony Lane, op.cit., p. 158–9.

[21] The main study is by Political and Economic Planning: *Advisory Committees in British Government* (George Allen and Unwin, London 1960).

[22] Walkland, op.cit., p. 50.

[23] TUC evidence to the Fulton Committee reprinted in the *TUC Report 1967*, p. 382..

[24] Ibid.

[25] See Samuel Brittan: *The Treasury Under the Tories* (Penguin, Harmondsworth 1964), and Harold Macmillan: *At the End of the Day* (Macmillan, London 1973).

[26] Some have suggested, though, that part of the eventual bargain on NEDC membership included a commitment to ease controls on pay. See, for example, Aubrey Jones: *The New Inflation* (Penguin, Harmondsworth 1973), p. 51; also Dorfman, op.cit., pp. 104—13.

[27] *TUC Report 1962*, p. 369. It is clear that some of the TUC's preferences were shared by both the Chancellor and the employers' representatives against the reservations of some in the Cabinet and the Treasury.

[28] Ibid., p. 254.

[29] *The Growth of the United Kingdom Economy to 1966* (HMSO, February 1963) and *Conditions Favourable to Faster Growth* (HMSO, April 1963).

[30] *TUC Report 1963*, p. 390.

[31] Ibid.

[32] Ibid.

[33] *Trade Unionism*, op.cit., p. 9.

[34] *TUC Report 1963*, p. 383 *et seq.* gives an account of the debate from which the quotations are taken.

[35] *TUC Report 1970*, p. 439, 1971 pp. 250 and 254–9, and 1973 p. 301.

[36] For an excellent summary of the development and work of the EDCs up to 1971 see G.D. Vaughan: 'Economic Development Committees' (*Public Administration,* vol. 49, Winter 1971).

[37] Supplementary Report, 'Economic Development and Planning', p. 11, reprinted in *TUC Report 1963*.

[38] Vaughan says that because of the employers' realisation of this possibility it required 'time and tact' to persuade them to support the establishment of EDCs (Vaughan, op.cit., p. 368).

[39] *TUC Report 1971*, pp. 267–9.

[40] *TUC Report 1961*, p. 376.

[41] See Macmillan, op.cit. and Brittan, op.cit.

42  *TUC Report 1971*, p. 257.

43  The TUC representatives on the NEDC attended meetings of the Labour Party's NEC in 1963 to discuss 'problems of economic planning, particularly planning for expansion' and whether these issues should continue to be discussed within the NEDC or the responsibility transferred to a new ministry. (*TUC Report 1963*, p. 267.)

44  '. . . the July [meeting] discussed the future of the NEDC and there was general agreement on the valuable role which the Council would continue to play.' (*TUC Report 1970*, p. 443.)

45  *TUC Report 1965*, p. 294.

46  *TUC Report 1972*, p. 249.

47  The quotation is from Edward Heath's broadcast following the end of the strike.

48  *TUC Report 1973*, p. 274.

49  For further discussion on the miners' strike and the issues it raised see chapter 5.

50  An interesting attempt to relate this lack of centralisation to the underlying characteristics of industrial structure in Britain can be found in Geoffrey K. Ingham: *Strikes and Industrial Conflict* (Macmillan, London 1974).

51  On the formation of the CBI see Stephen Blank, op cit. On its work and some of its internal difficulties see W.P. Grant and D. Marsh, op cit. and also 'The Politics of the CBI: 1974 and after' (*Government and Opposition*, vol. 10 [1], Winter 1975).

52  Quite apart from its own extremely sketchy organisational structure its claim to be the central body for the trade union movement was challenged both by the General Federation of Trade Unions and the Triple Alliance.

53  On this important period see V.L. Allen: 'The Re-organisation of the Trades Union Congress 1918–27', originally in *British Journal of Sociology*, 1960 and subsequently reprinted in Allen's *The Sociology of Industrial Relations* (Longman, London 1971).

54  The main sanction is expulsion from the TUC which involves the loss of certain benefits, of which the most important is likely to be the protection of the Bridlington Agreement on inter-union competition for members. But the seriousness of this will be subject to wide variation from union to union.

55  Sir Alec Cairncross, a former Economic Adviser to the Government, has said: 'The average worker's pay packet in Britain is fixed as to about half by wage agreements at national level between trade unions and employers associations. Most of the other half is settled within the plant.'

(*Three Banks Review* [100], December 1973, p. 17.)

56 John Corina: *The Labour Market: Part One of Incomes Policy — Problems and Prospects* (Institute of Personnel Management, London 1966), p. 12. Cf. Clegg's verdict on the war-time bargain: 'by increasing real earnings of manual workers at a time of rationing and high taxation it achieved the greatest advance towards economic equality that Britain has ever experienced in such a short period' (H.A. Clegg: *The System of Industrial Relations in Britain* [Basil Blackwell, Oxford 1972], p. 399).

57 The phrase comes from a discussion of the Conservative government's policies in this period by Lord Birkenhead in *Walter Monckton* (Weidenfeld and Nicolson, London 1969), chapter 27.

58 Nigel Fisher in commenting on Monckton's replacement by Iain Macleod says: 'Within one week of his arrival at the ministry he had impressed upon his staff that one of his main objectives was to bring wage inflation under close control.' (Nigel Fisher: *Iain Macleod* [André Deutsch] London 1973.)

59 The two most relevant statements in the Conservatives' 1970 Manifesto were: 'We utterly reject the philosophy of compulsory wage control' and 'Labour's compulsory wage control was a failure and we will not repeat it'.

60 Samuel Brittan talks of 'misunderstandings that arose during these talks' but the TUC's willingness to engage in them (in the person of Vic Feather, then the Assistant General Secretary) gives some credence to Harold Macmillan's comment on the TUC's condemnation of the NIC: 'there were a number of the more responsible leaders who said little and from whom I believed we could expect quiet and uneffusive sympathy' (Brittan, op.cit., p. 240. and Macmillan, op.cit., p. 108).

61 *TUC Report 1966*, p. 323.

62 *TUC Report 1973*, pp. 278 and 283 *et seq.*

63 *'Let's Go with Labour for the New Britain'*, Labour Party Election Manifesto 1964 reprinted in F.W.S. Craig (ed.): *British General Election Manifestos, 1918–1966* (Political Reference Publications, Chichester 1970).

64 Ibid.

65 Macmillan, op.cit., p. 44.

66 It would be too much to say that these are *necessary* features of any statutory policy, for various supporters of incomes policy have suggested ways in which they may be overcome, e.g. Hugh Clegg's *How to Run an Incomes Policy and Why We Made Such a Mess of the Last One* (Heinemann, London 1971), but these features have certainly been associated with the various policies attempted in Britain since 1945.

67  *TUC Report 1973*, p. 278.

68  This specific comment was made in response to the invitation of the Chairman of the Pay Board to comment on the Board's review of anomalies that had arisen during the freeze (i.e. Stage One of the Conservatives' statutory policy). Similarly the General Council made no comments on the consultative document that accompanied the initial publication of the Pay and Prices Code (Ibid., pp. 288–9).

69  A number of TUC statements have reflected this view of some of its members, e.g. 'Trade unionists are not interested in an incomes policy which is based on the assumption that the share of national income going to working people will remain the same. Their interest lies in a radical and progressive incomes policy which will increase their share in the nation's wealth' (*TUC Report 1967*, p. 325).

70  At the 1947 Labour Party Conference Arthur Deakin said: 'Under no circumstances will we accept the position that the responsibility for the fixation of the regulation of conditions of employment is one for the government' (quoted in Beer, op cit., p. 209).

71  At a joint conference organised by the Social Science Research Council and the National Institute of Economic and Social Research in January 1972 on the subject of incomes policy those trade unionists who did attend pointed out that they were not typical: '. . . most trade unionists would refuse to attend a conference about incomes policy. For the whole concept was now anathema to trade union leaders. This was because they had in the beginning supported incomes policy because they believed it would help faster real growth and assist the low paid. In fact it was identified in their minds with restriction, low growth and a flat or falling standard of living' (F. Blackaby [ed.]: *An Incomes Policy for Britain* [Heinemann, London 1972], p. 12).

72  *TUC Report 1965*, p. 466.

73  *TUC Report 1966*, p. 476. Author's italics.

74  *TUC Report 1965*, p. 487.

75  See, for example, *TUC Report 1968*, pp. 356–7 and the speeches of the CAWU and COHSE delegates at the 1967 Conference of Trade Union Executives (*Incomes Policy – Report of a Conference of Executive Committees of Affiliated Organisations, March 1967*, published by the TUC in that year).

76  The *TUC Report 1968* quotes a figure of 60 per cent of workers covered by claims notified to the vetting Committee for the period July 1967–May 1968 though it is unclear whether this means *all* workers or workers in unions affiliated to the TUC. By the time of the 1968 Congress support was only just retained for the vetting committee and the General

Council reported in 1969 that it had noted 'that there had been a significant fall in claim notifications' (*TUC Report 1969*, p. 433).

[77] Frank Blackaby comments that the Incomes Policy Committee was 'almost wholly ineffective' as an exercise in voluntary wage restraint (Blackaby, op.cit., p. 226) and Dorfman similarly talks of 'the complete failure of the Incomes Policy Committee' (Dorfman, op.cit., p. 138).

[78] *TUC Report 1967* (pp. 331–2) and *1968* (pp. 354 and 360).

[79] *TUC Report 1966*, p. 323.

[80] *TUC Report 1967*, pp. 331–2.

[81] 'Productivity agreements . . . were easier and quicker to negotiate with individual firms than with employers associations for whole trades or industries' (H.A. Turner: 'Collective Bargaining and the Eclipse of Incomes Policy: Retrospect, Prospect and Possibilities' *British Journal of Industrial Relations*, vol. 8, p. 204).

[82] For the debate see the *TUC Report 1969*.

[83] TUC: *Economic Policy and Collective Bargaining — Report of a Special Trades Union Congress*, March 1973, p. 20 (italics as in the original).

[84] Hughes and Pollins, op.cit., p. 19.

[85] The General Council's review is reprinted in their 'Report to Congress' (*TUC Report 1969*, p. 419 *et seq.*).

[86] *TUC Report 1968*, p. 502–4.

[87] Incomes Policy — Report of a Conference. . . p. 20.

[88] *TUC Report 1969*, op.cit.

[89] Alan Fisher, General Secretary of NUPE, in requesting a popular version of the 1968 Economic Review commented: '(it is) an excellent document but not very digestible so far as the rank and file of the movement are concerned' (*TUC Report 1968*, p. 510).

[90] *TUC Report 1968*, p. 561. A delegate did suggest to the 1969 Congress that it should debate and endorse the Economic Review since this might carry more weight with the government. But this has not been followed up, other than with the rather special case noted in note 91 below.

[91] *Economic Policy and Collective Bargaining — Report of a Special Trades Union Congress*, March 1973 (TUC, London 1973), p. 71. A full Congress was in fact substituted for the customary Conference of Union Executives to debate the Conservative government's Stage Two prices and incomes policy. The General Council's Report to the Congress largely comprised the 1973 Review with some recommendations for action tacked on the end.

[92] Ibid, p. 71.

[93] *TUC Report 1972*, p. 107.

# 5 Trade Unions and Direct Action

In conventional discussions of interest group strategies a third strategy is usually distinguished in addition to action through the Executive and through Parliament. It would perhaps be more correct to call it a collection of strategies for it ranges from public relations campaigns indiscriminately directed at the public to actions that involve breaking the law and the possibility of fines or imprisonment. There is a danger that grouping these strategies under the title direct action, as this chapter does, may confuse rather than illuminate but political scientists have not been very successful in coming forward with any clear and agreed definitions that would help us very much. A recent reader entitled *Direct Action and Democratic Politics*[1] which focused on Britain had to admit after a preliminary conference of some of its contributors the impossibility of agreeing on a common definition. Another recent contribution by April Carter to the study of direct action notes that it is 'a popular but somewhat ambiguous term' and that 'any strict definition in terms of goal, or of the persons using it is likely to become sterile or misleading'.[2] The author does however offer a useful classification of the techniques that can be employed by any group concerned with attempting to engineer change. The spectrum of possibilities stretches from constitutional action (which would embrace most of what we have looked at so far) through 'symbolic action' (e.g. marches, rallies, parades, fasts) and 'direct action' (strikes, boycotts, sit-ins, defiance of the law) to guerilla warfare and street fighting.

As Miss Carter's discussion makes clear, trade unions have been the historical pioneers of many forms of 'direct action'. However, in more recent times they have been replaced in both popular and academic interest by other groups — black protest groups in the USA, students, and anti-Vietnam and anti-nuclear weapons groups. Unions have of course continued to utilise the strike as an integral weapon in their collective bargaining strategy. What is of some novelty is that in recent years they have supplemented the strike by following the example of some of the newer protest groups with regard to tactics. Thus the sit-in has been quite widely used, usually in order to preserve jobs where the employer wished to enforce redundancies. Chapter 2 distinguished the main concerns that had driven trade unions to take political action and in the light of that discussion the aim of this chapter is to select some of the major examples in recent years where some form of direct action has been used. In choosing to focus on a limited number of cases one is necessarily ignoring some examples of the resort to direct action. Nevertheless, the hope is that by concentrating on the major examples many of the important issues which direct action raises will be illuminated. So far as the legal framework governing trade union activity is concerned we have indicated previously that a major part of the TUC's efforts have been directed at persuading sympathetic MPs and later the Labour Party to promise revision of the law when they are elected to office. However, in the period 1968–69 the unions were confronted with a Labour government that wished to change the law in certain directions to which the unions were strongly opposed. No help was likely from the Conservative Party, not only because trade unionists had little, if any, experience of enlisting that Party in the pursuit of their objectives, but also because it was already committed to the policies outlined in April 1968 in *Fair Deal at Work* which was seen by trade unionists as an unwelcome and hostile document. Despite the nature of the proposals contained in the Labour government's White Paper *In Place of Strife* and the fact that they were largely settled by the time the General Council saw the proposals, those Labour ministers most closely involved, namely Harold Wilson and Barbara Castle, were never unwilling to discuss them with the TUC. Indeed the rationale of the proposals has been presented by Harold Wilson in terms of using the threat of legislation to oblige the TUC to carry out a disciplining role within the trade union movement. There is no reason to doubt this since a similar logic prevailed with incomes policy developments in 1965 (see pp. 115–18). What *can* justifiably be doubted is whether the eventual conclusion of the affair was as satisfactory to Harold Wilson and Barbara Castle as they claimed at the time. Although the TUC may, as Wilson claimed, have moved further in a few weeks than in forty years, it certainly did not regard the agreement entered into on 18 June 1969 as conceding anything particularly vital. There were calls, particularly after the announcement of an early Bill by Roy Jenkins in his Budget Speech, for a one day national strike but this was rejected by the General Council.[3] It did concede the need for a Special Congress, the request for which had originally been made in February but which gathered irresistible force after the announcement of early legislation, but since the government was willing to continue talks with the General Council on the major principles which were embodied in the proposed legislation there appeared little need for supplementary action.

As Jenkins' account of *In Place of Strife* makes clear, the TUC's strategy under the leadership of Vic Feather had been to behave as the major group affected by the legislation and to attempt through a reasoned approach to persuade the Labour government to desist from its stated intentions. Neither the TUC nor individual unions allowed themselves to become deeply involved in the disputes within the PLP and the serious questions raised about the leadership of Harold Wilson. Since the eventual outcome seemed very satisfactory to the TUC it was not perhaps surprising that it should have felt that it would be able to employ a similar strategy with the Conservative government when it came into office in 1970. The TUC was obviously aware that in the shape of *Fair Deal at Work* the Conservative Party had produced an industrial relations policy which involved substantial changes in the legal framework and that it had a manifesto commitment to implement those proposals.[4] Nevertheless, there were important reasons for the TUC to doubt the seriousness of that commitment. In the first place there were good precedents for believing that commitments entered into in opposition are not necessarily carried out on the assumption of office. This of course applies not only to matters which involve trade unionists but the TUC did have something of a direct precedent in the 1946 Trade Disputes Act which the Conservative Opposition had declared it would reverse when it achieved power, though as it turned out this was never done. In the second place, the experience with post-war Conservative governments had been encouraging insofar as procedure was concerned, even when the substance of the policies had been objectionable. All the Conservative administrations between 1951 and 1964 had accorded the TUC considerable consultative rights on a wide range of policies. Thus six days after the General Election of 1970 the TUC issued a statement indicating that it expected the incoming Conservative government to maintain the practice of consultation.[5] It therefore seemed quite reasonable to the TUC to assume that it would be able to persuade the Conservative government to substantially modify, indeed perhaps wholly abandon, any proposed labour legislation. At the 1970 TUC Congress, after declaring their opposition to any such legislation, Vic Feather expressed the hope that the forthcoming consultative document promised by the government 'will be a genuine consultative document and that its proposals will be susceptible to change in response to reasoned argument' and concluded by anticipating that 'It may well be that we shall all have to embark again on another tedious process of educating the politicians about industry'.[6]

These more or less confident expectations were rudely shattered by the train of events that followed shortly upon the conclusion of the 1970

Congress. The government produced its consultative document at the beginning of October and attached to it a six week timetable which was designed to encompass all representations from interested parties. A meeting with the Secretary of State for Employment followed preliminary consideration by the General Council of the document. This was a crucial meeting since the government made it clear that the document contained 'eight central pillars' which 'it had no intention of removing', they were essentially 'non-negotiable provisions'.[7] These eight pillars contained the major innovations which the proposed Act would introduce and were, of course, all highly objectionable to the trade unions. The TUC countered by suggesting some tripartite discussions with the government and the CBI to seek for ways to improve the *voluntary* system of industrial relations, but the government was quite unsympathetic both to this and to the General Council's continued willingness for consultations provided that 'the government was open to persuasion on the merits of its central proposals'.[8] The government had made its position clear and the General Council was thus forced to consider alternative strategies. Before the main aspects of this campaign are discussed the importance of this government refusal to budge on the central provisions of its projected legislation should be emphasised. The implications for trade union behaviour of these proposals made the legislation highly objectionable but the government's insistence on the non-negotiable nature of the provisions added insult to injury. It was of considerable importance in hardening the resistance and increasing the general animosity towards the Conservative government of many right wing and moderate members of the General Council; both the language of the TUC's own account and the speeches of delegates at the Special Congress reveal this very clearly. The introduction to the General Council's report to the Special Congress talks of the 'wilful denial of the facilities for consultation that have been accorded the TUC by every government for at least the past thirty years'.[9] Alex Donnet, speaking for the NUGMW, the TUC's third largest affiliate and a consistently right wing union since 1945, declared that 'All British governments know or should know that consultation is of special importance and significance to the trade union movement because it expresses their members' desire that their representatives should have full and free opportunity of putting forward their views and having them considered before conclusions are reached'. [10]

The decision to launch a public campaign, given the government's unwillingness to yield on the central principles of the legislation, had two objectives. The first was largely internally orientated — to acquaint the mass of the trade unions' membership with what was objectionable about the Conservative proposals — and the second was directed at the general public 'in an attempt to persuade the government to reconsider its intentions'. [11] The means selected to implement these objectives suggest that the first rather than the second was the more important. This is not particularly surprising, given that it is unclear how one does mobilise public opinion in the undifferentiated way the second objective suggests and even less clear how public opinion effectively deflects a majority government from central parts of its legislative programme. The General Council was doubtless conscious of the fact that the most widely used measure of public opinion — the sample survey polls — had for some time indicated hostility to various aspects of trade union behaviour and support for the kind of measures proposed by both *In Place of Strife* and *Fair Deal at Work.* [12] However, worse than a public opinion which in aggregate displayed these views was the evidence that trade unionists as a particular section of that public were themselves apparently far from immune to such reactions as shown by their criticism of the unions to which they belonged and not averse either to many of the 'reform' proposals put forward in the 1960s. The logic of a public campaign therefore appeared to be to mobilise trade unionists behind the arguments of the General Council in order to demonstrate to the government that the interest group most affected by their proposals was unitedly opposed to them. When the General Council came to review the public campaign in April 1971 it felt able to conclude that its efforts 'had resulted in a substantial shift of opinion amongst trade unionists against the government's proposals'. [13]

This emphasis on demonstrating trade union opposition to measures that would particularly affect them is worth further comment because of its connections with the themes of parliamentary representation and functional representation previously referred to. The unions could not help but be aware that the Conservative government had been elected through the due processes of a General Election and that they had given a good indication of their intentions so far as labour legislation was concerned in their election manifesto. Inevitably, they were likely to claim that the election and the manifesto gave them a mandate for their legislation. This was an argument that worried some of the TUC leadership since they made a number of efforts to contest the claim that the Conservatives had such a mandate. Jack Jones claimed that the Conservatives had won their victory by their commitment to cut price rises and that far more people had *not* voted for the Conservatives than had voted for them. [14] Feather drew on another associated argument often used by those who wish to dispute mandate theory, namely that most of those who had voted Conservative had no idea (until the TUC publicity campaign told them) what the Conservative proposals really amounted to.[15] But one of the main grounds that justified trade union resistance to the Conservative proposals was undoubtedly the corpus of beliefs that has been previously distinguished by the concept of 'functional representation'. In the case of the Industrial Relations Act it amounts to saying that as the trade unions were one of the most important interests involved, some would say *the* most important, they had both a special competence and special rights with regard to such legislation. It would certainly be relevant to ask how representative the central body of the trade unions, the TUC, was when deciding on whether such competence and rights should be recognised, but in no way was it relevant how substantial a section of the general electorate the TUC constituted. It happens to be a large section, but if one was dealing with medical decisions the BMA, which is miniscule in relation to the electorate, would similarly be entitled to special rights and consideration. This line of reasoning amounted to saying in the case of the Industrial Relations Act that, whatever the results of a general election might appear to indicate, such legislation should on the strongest interpretation be abandoned or, slightly less affirmatively, that major concessions of principle should be made to the trade union viewpoint.

However widely these kind of views were held by trade unionists, the difficulties of accommodating functional and parliamentary representation were raised even more acutely when the unions tried to agree on what their strategy of opposition should be. The Conservative government was not willing to accept the implications of functional representation if it meant any concessions on the major principles of the Industrial Relations Act. Some trade unionists believed that however discouraging the parliamentary situation might appear to be, with the Conservative Party having a majority over all other parties, an attempt should be made to prevent the passage of the legislation. A Liaison Committee for the Defence of Trade Unions had been created some years before to oppose statutory controls on prices and incomes. It had strong links with the Communist Party, though the support embraced many who were not, and never had been, party members. The Committee succeeded in assembling 1,800 delegates in November 1970 for what was described as 'the largest unofficial conference ever held'.[16] Although a call for a general strike was defeated, the conference agreed to hold a one day strike on 8 December and to demand TUC official backing for it. This was refused by the TUC which condemned the strike and its eventual support was not very impressive.[17]

The major rank and file resistance to the Bill came from the same occupational sectors and the relevant unions who had been most strongly opposed to the Labour government's *In Place of Strife*. Both Conservative and Labour governments agreed that the industrial relations 'problem' was more acute in some sectors than in others and accordingly that the practical effect of their measures appeared to threaten the existing rights of some trade unionists much more than others. The AUEW and TGWU were the two unions most directly involved and those that came under most pressure to take action to defeat the Bill. The leaders of these two unions attempted to persuade the TUC to back a one day strike in February but were easily out-voted. [18] The AUEW organised two one day strikes against the Bill on 1 and 18 March, the latter coinciding with the day of the TUC's own Special Congress. Despite divisions among the union's leadership, both the strikes received considerable support from the membership. The TGWU constructed a somewhat ambiguous formula by regarding both occasions as 'non-cooperation days', though it did back the 18 March strike in the engineering and shipbuilding industries. The logic of this one day strike activity was not altogether clear, although some clues were provided by the AUEW's President, Hugh Scanlon, when he spoke at the Special Congress. Although some of his remarks seemed to urge an indefinite programme of strikes 'to bring about, if necessary, the defeat of the government', the more significant rationale of strikes was suggested by the idea that if the TUC agreed on a programme of industrial action it would 'create an atmosphere certainly for more realistic discussion and certainly, in my view, for considerable concessions which have not been forthcoming in any of our meetings with the government'. [19] Earlier in the same speech Scanlon had deplored what he called 'the defeatist view that the Bill must of necessity become an Act', but some three months before this he had himself appeared to accept that the Bill would be passed. [20] His apparently more militant stance in March may have reflected a build-up of opposition within his union but it seems likely that he was still accepting that the Conservative Party would put some kind of Industrial Relations Act on the statute book but that there remained a possibility of some concessions if the strike weapon was deployed under TUC auspices.

The TUC, however, had not only to respond to the pressure of the TGWU and AUEW for advancing beyond its own campaign which had eschewed strike action, but also to the real possibility that many of its affiliates would comply with the Bill when it finally became an Act. If they were likely to behave in this way then it made it very unlikely that they would support any action that went much beyond the TUC's use of conventional protest tactics — petitions, marches, mass leafleting, national newspaper advertising, and the like. The concern with trying to bridge the divisions in the TUC and thus to find the oppositional strategy that would command general assent were evident in the General Council's report to the Special Congress. The divisiveness of strike action was made the main grounds for rejecting the report rather than any scruples about utilising the industrial strength of the movement to pressurise a government, though delegates did also say that *if* such strikes did take place they thought this would strengthen rather than weaken the government's resolve.

The TUC may certainly have been correct in thinking that a strike sponsored by itself against the Bill would have strengthened the government's determination to get its legislation on the statute book. What is less clear is whether they would have been able to continue to govern with much effectiveness if a total or partial strike had been mounted against the Bill. One is bound to raise this possibility in the light of the two coal strikes of 1972 and 1974 and the indeterminacy of the February 1974 General Election in which the authority of the government was one of the central issues. Nevertheless, a series of one day strikes backed by the TUC or, even more, an unlimited strike would have been a much more explicit political challenge to the government than was the case with either of the two miners' strikes which arose from wage bargaining. Although the General Council itself refrained from giving this as a reason for its reluctance to endorse industrial action, a number of General Council members made the point quite explicit in the debate that took place at the Special Congress. [21] Where the General Council was quite justified was in assuming that any call for industrial action would *not* have met with a united response. Various unions made it quite clear at the Special Congress that the members would not respond to a call for such action and that the consequences of such a policy would do considerable damage to certain individual unions. [22] On this issue, too, some of the advocates of industrial action seem to have generalised from rather slim evidence on the response that could be expected from the TUC's membership and the impact that this would have. Thus Eddie Marsden of the Construction Section of the AUEW acknowledged that industrial action would involve difficulties for some unions but declared on the basis of the response to the AUEW's strikes of 1 and 18 March that 'the vast majority, certainly the active sections of the movement' would support it. Those strikes *did* demonstrate that the 'active sections' of the AUEW were willing to support industrial action but, as has been pointed out, they were among the most vulnerable to the alterations embodied in the projected legislation. Percy Coldrick similarly rebuked Danny

McGarvey's implied suggestion that the support for the February demonstration in London could be taken as evidence of a general willingness among the TUC affiliated membership to take further action.

The other major point of contention at the Special Congress reflected the main strategy that the TUC had developed for opposing the Bill. This strategy accepted that the Bill would become an Act but sought to pursue a policy of non-cooperation in its implementation. In addition to not recognising the various agencies established by the Act, the TUC's main objective was to persuade unions not to register under the Act. If they were successful in this attempt the Act would be seriously prejudiced since it was an important part of its rationale that the vast majority of unions would register. However, the prospects of successfully holding all its affiliates to the policy of non-registration (which was a perfectly legal option) did not seem very much brighter than for mobilising them for industrial action. The General Council had formulated a proposition that 'strongly advised unions not to register' but shied away from more affirmative terms such as 'instructs'. This formula received the approval of the Special Congress [23] but the debate made it clear that the formula was far too weak in the eyes of some (for instance, the TGWU, UPW and ACTT) and too strong in the view of others (NALGO and the NUT). Fortunately, events helped to resolve some of the divisions in the following eighteen months — initially the prospects of a damaging split among affiliated unions appeared to increase when the AUEW succeeded at the September 1971 Conference in strengthening the line on registration by substituting 'instructs' for the more permissive formula originally approved, [24] but events during the spring and summer of 1972 seemed to confirm not only the analysis of the Industrial Relations Act as 'class-based' legislation deliberately designed to weaken the organised working class movement, but also the more moderate analysis that the Act would not improve but actually worsen the climate of industrial relations. The TGWU was fined £55,000, the cooling-off and compulsory ballot provisions were invoked against the NUR to little visible benefit and finally in July 1972 five London dockers found themselves in gaol as an indirect result of the Act. [25] This imprisonment produced spontaneous strike action among a number of groups of workers and after an abortive meeting with the Prime Minister the General Council called a national one day strike. As the dockers were soon released this one day strike did not take place but it seems very likely that it would have been widely observed and that many unions would have prolonged the action whether or not the TUC had been willing to extend its own commitment.

The net result was that by the time of the 1972 Annual Congress only thirty-two unions with a total of half a million members were suspended from the TUC and the final act of expulsion in the following year involved a further reduction from 32 to 20 unions, representing some 353,000 of Congress' 10 million affiliated membership. [26] Only four unions of any size were represented — the National Union of Seamen (43,000); the Bakers' Union (50,000); NUBE (103,000) and COHSE (113,000). Thus aided by events, the AUEW's 1971 resolution substituting 'instruct' for 'advise' had been very nearly wholly successful in preventing TUC compliance with a central provision of the Act. However, subsequent attempts to build upon this were not similarly successful and indicate the additional difficulties many unions have when faced with disobeying the law, however substantial their objection to the essence of what the law represents. Throughout the life of the Industrial Relations Act the AUEW was consistent in opposing the Act in its entirety, refusing even to appear in a defensive role at the NIRC even after a TUC decision in favour of this. Indeed, the union believed that the decision, which had been made by the General Council, was inconsistent with the decisions of the 1971 Special Congress and Annual Congress and hence put forward a motion at the 1972 Congress to make such appearances impossible (insofar as a TUC resolution could do this). Both those in favour and those opposed drew on historical evidence. Feather chose to emphasise that previous laws the unions had opposed had been reversed through political parliamentary action, for example, the reversal of Taff Vale, the 1927 Trade Disputes Act and the effects of the *Rookes* v. *Barnard* judgement. Both Scanlon and Harry Urwin, speaking for the TGWU, believed that industrial action had an important role to play, Scanlon citing the release of the dockers who had been imprisoned the previous July and Urwin the part played by industrial action in the combined industrial and political campaigns which had reversed previous anti-union legislation. In reply to Feather's insistence that 'trade unionists respect the rule of law', Urwin arued that trade unionists did not accept 'bad law' and a similar theme was struck by H. Elvin of the ACTT who said that 'people of conscience have defied evil Acts of Parliament throughout the centuries and this is certainly an evil Act of Parliament and should be defied'. [27]

Although the AUEW and the TGWU were able to obtain the support of a number of other unions, the majority endorsed the General Council's decision to allow unions to defend themselves before the NIRC. [28] The important difference between non-registration as a tactic and refusal to appear before the NIRC was that the former, as has been previously pointed out, was a quite legal option, whereas the latter was virtually certain to involve the union in the question of contempt of court and thus

108

illegal action. Furthermore, the size of the fine imposed on the TGWU in March 1972 had indicated that in addition to the financial costs which were likely to flow from de-registered status, the unions could also be involved in escalating fines as a result of their refusal to appear before the NIRC. Nevertheless, despite the unwillingness of the majority of the unions to engage in action against the Industrial Relations Act which clearly involved a clash with the law, the willingness of unions such as the AUEW to run such risks served to substantially discredit the Act. Although other unions were not prepared to sanction TUC support for such activity, they were prepared, on the precedent of the dockers, to resort to strike action in defence of trade unionists who had tangled with the law when it involved imprisonment. There may have been many reservations about the precise rights and wrongs of the issue that led to the imprisonment of the five dockers but the response to this sentence demonstrated that such reservations were over-ridden by the nature of the penalty exacted. Both this incident and the subsequent problems the AUEW faced through its refusal to attend the NIRC could be, and were, used to emphasise the general TUC case that at the level of pragmatic commonsense observation the Industrial Relations Act did not make for an improvement but, on the contrary, for a marked worsening in the climate of industrial relations. Thus the difficulties of arriving at a common position on the best strategy and tactics for opposing the Act did not prevent the trade union movement from opposing it, possibly in the most effective way from the point of view of achieving its suspension or abolition. For in terms of functional representation, the TUC policy of de-registration demonstrated that, contrary to many predictions, the movement was virtually united in its opposition to a central feature of the legislation. It is a reflection of the success of the TUC's policy that when Campbell Adamson, Director General of the CBI, declared that the Industrial Relations Act had soured the whole climate of industrial relations, Edward Heath believed that this had been a vital factor in his defeat in the February 1974 General Election. Adamson was as aware as many others that the 'souring' was a result of trade union refusal to co-operate with the Act but his conclusion that this refusal must be accepted as a fact of life and that substantial modifications to the Act were thus needed is an important testament to the efficacy of trade union strategy.

The other major area in which the debate about an appropriate strategy has involved a discussion of the possibilities of direct action relates, of course, to prices and incomes policies. It was emphasised in chapter 2 how the pervasive concern by governments since 1945, and especially from the

1960s onwards, with the level of wage settlements has meant great difficulties for unions who wish for untrammelled free collective bargaining with employers. The various responses to the successive incomes policies were examined and it was seen that the main trade union response was to try to persuade government ministers to refrain from interfering and, where this was unsuccessful (as it frequently was), to minimise the impact of statutory controls on free collective bargaining. It was clear that with an enlarged public sector, even without statutory controls, many unions were negotiating with the State and thus with the government of the day.

The extent to which this situation became visible depended upon the different structures within the public sector. Services organised directly by government departments were the most visible (for example, the Post Office until 1969), public corporations rather less so and local authorities probably least of all. The Trade Disputes Act of 1946 has removed some of the ambiguities that surrounded the right of civil servants to take industrial action as well as allowing them to affiliate to the TUC. Similarly, employees of public corporations and local authorities were allowed, indeed actively encouraged, to join trade unions. [29] In the light of this it is perhaps surprising that relatively few negotiations in the past thirty years have developed to a point where the authority of government has been challenged. The potential for this kind of situation to develop seems considerable, particularly if one takes a highly unionised area in the public sector with a strong market situation and the operation of a statutory incomes policy.

These were in fact the essential ingredients that led to the miners' strike of February 1974. Almost exactly two years before a similar strike had taken place but there was at that time no *statutory* policy in force. There was at that time a widely held belief that the government was attempting to de-escalate the size of settlements, particularly in the public sector. The government maintained that the National Coal Board was a 'free agent' but the Board maintained that no more money was available and the government thus became indirectly involved. Unlike the private sector, where, if a company declares that there is no more cash available there is no 'fall-back position', [30] in the public sector the government always *does* represent such a court of final appeal. Furthermore, in a dispute which appears deadlocked, as between employers and employees, and has an important effect on the general state of the economy, there is very strong pressure on a government to mediate or to provide the machinery for such action. Thus in 1972 the impact of a well-organised national strike in which the NUM certainly saw the government as the relevant bargaining

110

unit and which led to widespread economic disruption, was brought to an end by a Court of Inquiry which eventually conceded most of what the NUM had been demanding.

The parties to this strike drew various conclusions from its success. For the NUM it was their first national strike since 1926 and in marked contrast to it in its almost complete success. It brought to public attention a shift in the political direction of the NUM and demonstrated that, although greatly reduced in size, it clearly still occupied an important strategic role in the economy. Other trade unions were given evidence of what a well-organised national strike could achieve, particularly if it received the sympathetic support of other relevant unions (e.g. in not crossing picket lines). It was seen by the government as a defeat for its concern to keep the level of wage settlements on a de-escalating path and did not improve its general authority, particularly when it was obliged to make further concessions to the NUM which were not wholly met by the Court of Inquiry. The public posture of the government was to suggest that some alternative means of meeting potential conflicts must be found. The strike served to rehabilitate the trade union movement as a serious interest that could do severe damage to a central part of the government's strategy. The government had pursued its aims for reforming industrial relations without taking into account trade union objections, for it knew that to do so would mean sacrificing most, if not all, of the major principles involved. Whether that legislation would succeed or not was not yet clear but, on the evidence of the miners' strike, sufficient economic damage could be done (both directly through the strike and indirectly through the wage norms it established for other groups to aim at) to make it imperative for the government to try to establish on what terms some kind of 'deal' could be struck. This was the essential background to the tripartite talks which have been discussed previously.

Similarly, we have seen that although there was strong opposition to the introduction of statutory controls by the Conservative government, there was also considerable difficulty in formulating an agreed programme of action. When strategy was debated at the Special Congress in March 1973 some unions wished to mount a TUC campaign against the statutory incomes legislation which involved industrial action. Although the original General Council recommendations were stiffened by imposing upon the Council a stronger co-ordinating role when unions found themselves in conflict with Stage Two, plus an obligation to organise a national day of protest and stoppages, this did not receive unanimous support. Many of those who did vote for it voted for a further motion which would have strengthened still further the TUC role in connection with unions in dispute. The intention of this latter motion was to try to ensure that any individual union which disputed the kind of wage settlement the statutory policy allowed for could depend upon the TUC to pursue its case. The motion was rejected, but not overwhelmingly — 3,280,000 voting in favour and 4,585,000 against.

A number of public sector unions who believed on the past precedent of incomes policy that they would be badly hit by such a policy were prominently associated with the motion. It was seconded by the ATTI but Bill Kendall of the CPSA believed that the ostensible commitment of the General Council to support unions who experienced difficulties with Stage Two was likely to amount to little or nothing, given the General Council's refusal to organise a conference of public sector unions in 1972. [31] But the public sector unions were not united; both NALGO and UPW and the EETU/PTU (with many members in the public sector) condemned the idea of industrial action. The latter two unions along with the POEU and APEX clearly believed that a preferable strategy was to work for the return of a Labour government and given this preference, industrial action was not only undesirable but also likely to be counterproductive. Roy Grantham told the Congress that 'A general strike will not end Phase Two or topple this government' [32] and although Frank Chapple considered that industrial action might force the Conservatives into an early election, it was not certain that the Labour Party would win in such circumstances, nor that if they did they could manage for long without a statutory policy. Chapple was somewhat isolated in making the latter suggestion but a number of those who were opposed to statutory controls emphasised the importance of the TUC itself attempting to devise a credible and enforceable policy. In his concluding remarks Vic Feather could only emphasise to the delegates who had made this kind of request that 'the TUC can deliver what you will agree the General Council shall deliver, not what the General Council agrees'. [33]

The predominant mood of the Congress was certainly not conducive to the working-out of a TUC alternative pay policy; it was primarily concerned with registering hostility to the government and the forlorn attempt to achieve some consensual basis for an oppositional strategy. The TUC interpretation of the 'middle' motion sponsored by the AUEW and the TGWU was to suggest that each affiliated union should choose its own means of protest and predictably, in the light of the earlier dissension and in the absence of a more positive lead by the General Council, the day fell far short of a national stoppage. By this time the General Council were involved with the government in 'talks about talks' on the possibilities for Stage Three of the prices and incomes policy. Although the contacts were

112

tentative and hesitant, [34] the talks represented a return to the established strategy of trying to influence government and although industrial action was not necessarily incompatible with this, it was probably not seen as a very effective way to influence the contents of successive stages of the policy.

No real success was achieved by the General Council in the attempt to persuade the government to return to a system of free collective bargaining when the Stage Three proposals were announced. [35] The proposals did in fact represent a response by the Government to demands that Stage Three should be more flexible than Stage Two, which would have the effect of giving more freedom to the bargaining agents, employers and employees. Nevertheless, this greater freedom had still to operate in a framework in which the maximum percentage and monetary figures were clearly delimited. Furthermore, although the controls on prices were the most extensive outside wartime experience, they did not amount to a freeze and the price of imported fresh food was not subject to any control.

As it turned out, Stage Three was destroyed some four months after it had been announced by the result of the February 1974 General Election which allowed the Labour Party to assume office. [36] This election was precipitated by the second national miners' strike within two years and illustrates vividly the conditions sketched out earlier for a confrontation between unions and government − a well organised union in the public sector with a strong bargaining position forced to negotiate within the confines of a statutory policy. It is not easy so close to these events either to give a very satisfactory account of circumstances that led to the election, or to say with any confidence what will be the medium and long term consequences of the result. Nevertheless, it seems difficult to deny that the Election did mark an important point in the relationships between government and unions and a number of the issues it raised are relevant to the themes pursued in this chapter. Three points in particular are worth discussing in some detail: the first concerns the sense in which the miners' strike was political rather than industrial; the second involves a consideration of the authority a government can mobilise against a determined and strategically placed sectional interest; and the third echoes one of the general themes of this book, namely the relationship between the TUC and its individual affiliates.

When an individual union finds itself constrained by an employer's stance which gives it less than it is prepared to settle for, the union normally engages in a progressive strategy of sanctions. For a union in the public sector the employer is in the last resort the government and although this means that sanctions are taken against the government, both parties for the most part follow the model provided by private enterprise and eventually reach some kind of accommodation. Neither the government nor the union see the conflict in terms of a *general* challenge to the government's authority but rather as a self-contained dispute between employer and employees over wages and conditions of work. This position is hard to maintain, however, when a government adopts a statutory incomes policy and promotes this policy as a central part of its economic strategy. This was precisely the position the Conservative government found itself in with regard to Stage Three. Mindful of the previous defeat inflicted by the NUM and the consequent difficulties this had led to within the Conservative Party, the government took steps to sound out the NUM on what would constitute an acceptable settlement *before* the Stage Three regulations were finalised. [37] Unfortunately the judgements made turned out to be wrong, even though the Stage Three limitations were very obviously designed with groups like the mineworkers principally in mind. Though there is some evidence that a section of the NUM executive did see the conflict that developed as a result of the rejection of the Stage Three offer as an opportunity to remove the Conservative government and thus any statutory restriction of wages, this was a minority view. The view of the majority of the executive and almost certainly of the rank and file was that more money was needed than the maximum that could be made available under Stage Three and that the union was thus engaged in an *industrial* conflict of classic dimensions. The government for its part could hardly help but see the conflict in political terms, that is, as a direct challenge to its authority since what was being disputed was a central plank in its current economic programme. The government saw any kind of compromise that involved finding special grounds for the miners that were not provided for in the Stage Three formula as greatly undermining, if not destroying, government credibility both within the Conservative Party and throughout the country generally. The dispute articulated in a way that few had since 1945 the difficulties of trying to reconcile the competing views of representation to which we have repeatedly drawn attention. The Conservative government *was* the duly elected government, notwithstanding that it was not the choice of the *majority* of the electorate [38] and that statutory control of prices and incomes had been explicitly *dis*avowed in the manifesto that brought it to office. [39] The NUM was a trade union with a very high membership density; it was not satisfied with the prescribed limits of Stage Three and, particularly after the oil crisis of October 1973, it occupied a very strong bargaining position.

114

In a situation of this kind the conventional wisdom assumed that such a conflict could be resolved by a general election. The logic of such an argument was that although conflicts between sectional interests and the government were not new, they were normally resolved by a measure of compromise by both parties to the dispute. If this was not possible, then the implicity superior authority of a government could be made explicit by the formal process of a general election. This would not, of course, resolve the conflict since the group with its demands would still be there to be dealt with after the election was concluded. But, as Edward Heath put it, there was the hope that it would create 'a completely different political situation'. [40] While Heath himself did not elaborate on this remark, many who sympathised with it believed that a decisive vote for the Conservative government would have considerably weakened the refusal of the miners to settling within the confines of Stage Three. However, given the fact that Heath had announced the referral of the miners' claim to the relativities machinery, this made the election less of a clear-cut choice between a trade union sectional demand and the authority of a government, since the government seemed tacitly to have given ground. Nevertheless, though this concession had been made, the relativities machinery was part of the statutory policy and Heath and the Cabinet presumably felt that an electoral endorsement of their conduct would enable Stage Three in particular, and the statutory policy generally, to be maintained. In the previous miners' strike in 1972 the Wilberforce recommendations and the further 'bidding up' by the NUM in direct negotiations with the Prime Minister had been the signal for a breakdown of the government's preferred course for wage movements. If a concession had again to be made to the miners then, providing it was made through the machinery of Stage Three designed specifically for special cases (however these might be determined), and providing the government's authority was endorsed by a favourable General Election verdict, the statutory policy could still be preserved with some semblance of credibility.

Such a verdict was, however, not forthcoming. It is more than usually difficult to know what significance *can* be read into the results of the poll beyond the rather negative factor that Heath's call for a strong majority did not evoke the response he wished for. The Conservatives appeared to have 'lost' the election, though it was far from clear that the Labour Party, or anyone else, had 'won' it. But this apparent refusal by the electorate to endorse the authority of a government in conflict with a major sectional interest is of considerable importance for it clearly puts some major question marks against the conventional wisdom that we have identified. The main source for evidence of popular opinion is inevitably the opinion polls with all their known limitations. Nevertheless, what they generally do appear to have shown was a degree of confusion and uncertainty which at the behavioural level seems to have been reflected by the electoral result. On the one hand the statutory policy on wages was widely supported and the importance of inflation acknowledged; but equally there was considerable support for the miners' claim. [41] It was also clear that as the campaign period progressed the issue of 'who governs', as it was cryptically referred to by many newspapers and politicians, lost ground as the major issue. This was true for both the voters, [42] the politicians, and the mass media.

As had always been realised, general elections, even where called on one issue, are difficult to limit, but this realisation had probably not been fully taken into account by those who had espoused the conventional wisdom about the appeal that could be made by a government against the demands of a particular group. Obviously there are a host of possible *caveats* that could be entered to any idea that the February Election failed to indicate the superior appeal of government. Many within the Conservative Party itself had doubts about whether the miners were the best group to tangle with, given their strong bargaining position and a generalised public sympathy for the nature of their work. Others, including Heath himself in the election post-mortem, argued that particular accidents in the campaign damaged the Conservatives sufficiently to prevent a strong endorsement of their appeal. [43] Here again, governments can only control the course of events both within and without the campaign period to a limited extent and the result of the February 1974 election will have emphasised this limitation to any future government tempted to follow the Conservatives' example. In fact it seems that one of the major consequences of the experience of the miners' strike and the ensuing General Election is to emphasise how undesirable it is for a government to find itself in the position the Conservatives did in February 1974. Though one may judge the results of the General Election as highly ambiguous, it has certainly damaged the idea that a government is bound to win in any conflict with a sectional group and thus underlined the necessity of trying to avoid getting into that position in the first place. This is bound to mean that the potential for particular unions — and possible also the TUC — to exercise influence has increased as a result. Government will more than ever wish to know what terms can be negotiated in order to try to avoid a major conflict of the kind clearly represented by the events of 1974.

This brings us to the third point that arises in a discussion of the general

116

significance of the conflict between the Conservative government and the NUM. This concerns the relationship between affiliated unions and the TUC, a theme constantly stressed in previous chapters. We have noted that a Special Congress was summoned to discuss Stage Two of the Conservatives' statutory policy and resulted in a formula which exhorted affiliated unions to participate in a day of protest against the legislation. Although the TUC took part in talks with the government about the shape of Stage Three the eventual proposals were condemned by the TUC. No further Special Congress was summoned, however, and the TUC's own strategy of opposition consisted of continuing efforts to persuade the government that it should change its policies and adopt the alternatives suggested by the TUC's 1973 Economic Review. However, it was more or less inevitable, given all the precedents, that when one of its affiliated members came into conflict with the policy it would fairly rapidly be drawn into the controversy. This was made even more certain when the government announced before Christmas that a three day week would be instituted from 1 January 1974 in order to conserve energy supplies. A major TUC initiative which developed from the Economic Committee of the General Council was put forward at the monthly NEDC meeting on 9 January. The initiative took the form of an assurance by the TUC that other unions would not use any exceptional settlement of the miners' dispute as a precedent in their own wage bargaining. This echoed very closely the formula the TUC had offered some twelve months before in a dispute in the health service but it had attracted far less attention since the context was much less critical than that of January 1974. [44]

The difficulties that the initiative presented were clear to many. It did not indicate acceptance of the statutory pay policy or of the particular details of Stage Three and there was still the perennial issue of how far the TUC could guarantee the terms of what it was offering (which did not in fact seem to amount to very much). The government's initial response was hostile but the TUC persisted with its offer and two meetings were held with Mr Heath. However, it was not possible to make any substantive progress. Though the government apparently believed that the TUC's proposal was more a matter of political manoeuvring and therefore not a very serious effort to resolve the strike, [45] there is some reason to believe that this was not actually the case. Sir Sidney Greene, the Chairman of the Economic Committee, was responsible for the initiative and his known moderate politics and commitment to a close and continuing relationship with government suggests that he certainly would have liked to propose a solution which could have satisfied all the parties to the conflict. However, given the government's narrow range for manoeuvre in terms of having to satisfy its own supporters and maintain some credibility for its policy, what it needed from the TUC was 'an explicit copper-bottomed guarantee that all other unions would adhere to the incomes policy as laid down' [46] and this the TUC could not provide. Fortunately perhaps for the TUC, its weakness in relation to its affiliated unions was at the time less obvious than the peremptory dismissal of its initiative by the Chancellor of the Exchequer, Anthony Barber. Len Murray was thus able to appear as a person offering a possible solution and, given the divided, not to say schizophrenic, nature of public attitudes towards the conflict, the TUC was certainly not discredited but probably enhanced as a participant in the dispute. What the outcome of the election demonstrated was rather similar to the campaign against the Industrial Relations Bill; because of the wide spectrum of views on the legislation, the TUC adopted a strategy that did not fully satisfy all its affiliated unions. In the case of the Industrial Relations Act the AUEW in particular went beyond TUC strategy but, far from undermining the TUC's position, the consequent conflicts provided important reinforcing evidence for the TUC's own pragmatic judgement that the Industrial Relations Bill worsened rather than improved the climate of industrial relations. Similarly, in the case of the statutory incomes policy, the TUC, although clearly opposed to both principle and detail of Stage Three, had no intention of using industrial action to challenge the policy. However, when the NUM did so decide, the TUC was both able to support the claim for the mineworkers to be treated again as a 'special case' [47] and at the same time to appear to be striving for a solution that would avoid the necessity for an all-out strike and the consequent dislocation. The position of the NUM was a particular illustration of the TUC's general case that statutory policies made for rigidities and inflexibilities and inhibited the orderly settlement of disputes between employers and employees. As a result of the General Election and the formation of the minority Labour government, the TUC position was greatly enhanced insofar as it was now in a position to exercise considerable influence on that government. During the campaign Harold Wilson emphasised the role of the social contract and despite, indeed perhaps because of, equivocation on the part of Hugh Scanlon as to its existence, Len Murray strongly asserted that such an understanding *did* exist.[48]

We have endeavoured in this chapter to examine in what sense the trade unions have employed direct action as a strategy in recent years. The discussion has been centred on the campaigns against *In Place of Strife* and the Industrial Relations Bill/Act of 1971, and the campaigns, covert or explicit, against incomes policies, in the period 1972–74. Most trade unionists recognise a distinction between industrial action for *industrial* objectives and industrial action for *political* objectives. There are considerable inhibitions so far as the latter is concerned and it was only in relation to the imprisonment of the five London dockers that the General Council endorsed a call for a general strike, though that phrase was *not* used and the action was intended to last for only twenty-four hours. Considerable disagreements have been displayed in relation to the role of industrial action by different unions and this has been reflected in the actual behaviour of unions confronted, for example, with the judgements of the NIRC. These differences relate partly to the differential impact of particular policies and to the different attitudinal and behavioural characteristics of particular unions. Where individual unions have engaged in direct action it appears both to have furthered their own objectives and to have reinforced the general opposition of the TUC, articulated through more conventional channels.

## Notes

[1]  R. Benewick and T. Smith (eds): *Direct Action and Democratic Politics* (George Allen and Unwin, London 1972).

[2]  April Carter: *Direct Action and Liberal Democracy* (Routledge and Kegan Paul, London 1973), p. 3.

[3]  *TUC Report 1969*, pp. 202–25. This contains a detailed account of the proposals of the government, the TUC's counter-proposals and the large number of meetings between the government and the General Council of the TUC between January and June 1969.

[4]  'We will introduce a comprehensive Industrial Relations Bill in the first session of the new Parliament. It will provide a proper framework of law within which improved relationships between management, men and unions can develop' (*A Better Tomorrow*, Conservative Party Manifesto 1970).

[5]  This statement is quoted in 'Chronicle, May–August 1970' *British Journal of Industrial Relations* vol. 8 [3], November 1970, p. 429.

[6]  *TUC Report 1970*, p. 576.

[7]  *TUC Report 1971*, p. 346. This account of the government's intentions and the General Council's reactions is also to be found in 'Report to Congress Part 1' in the *Industrial Relations Bill — Report of the Special Trades Union Congress 1971* (TUC, London 1971) pp. 3–11.

[8]  Ibid.

[9]  *TUC Report 1971*, p. 341.

[10]  *The Industrial Relations Bill – Report of the Special Trades Union Congress 1971*, op.cit., p. 64.

[11]  *TUC Report 1971*, p. 347.

[12]  See, for example, the summary in Jenkins, op.cit., pp. *xiii-xiv.*

[13]  *TUC Report 1971*, p. 99.

[14]  *The Industrial Relations Bill – Report of the Special Trades Union Congress 1971*, op.cit., pp. 54–5.

[15]  Ibid., p. 46.

[16]  *The Sunday Observer*, 5 December 1970, p. 6.

[17]  Estimates of the numbers involved varied between 350,000 and 600,000 ('Chronicle' *British Journal of Industrial Relations*, vol. 8, no. 1, February 1971). Taking the highest estimate, this means the strike was supported by approximately 6 per cent of trade unionists affiliated to the TUC.

[18]  At a Finance and General Purposes committee meeting on 4 February 1971 their proposal was defeated by seven votes to two (*Financial Times*, 5 February 1971, p. 36).

[19]  *The Industrial Relations Bill – Report of the Special Trades Union Congress 1971*, op.cit., p. 74.

[20]  *The Sunday Times*, 6 December 1970.

[21]  See especially the speeches of Frank Chapple and Jack Peel.

[22]  NALGO, APEX and NUPE all spoke in these terms.

[23]  The voting was 5,366,000 in favour and 3,992,000 against.

[24]  The motion was passed by 5,625,000 to 4,500,000 and the relevant section read 'Congress therefore instructs the General Council to support all unions in their fight against this legislation and to immediately instruct affiliated unions: (a) not to register under the Industrial Relations Act; (b) to take measures to remove themselves from the provisional register'.

[25]  They were actually gaoled for contempt of court but this contempt resulted from their refusal to comply with rulings of the National Industrial Relations Court which was a central part of the machinery of the Industrial Relations Act.

[26]  *TUC Report 1973*, pp. 102–3, 433 and 703. Membership figures have been provided to nearest '000.

[27]  This debate is given in *TUC Report 1972*, pp. 424–41.

[28]  The vote was 3,479,000 in favour of the AUEW motion, 5,677,000 against, a defeat of over two million votes.

[29]  George Bain has emphasised the important role of Government action in promoting the growth of white-collar unionism (George Sayers Bain: *The Growth of White-collar Unionism* [Clarendon Press, Oxford 1970]; see especially chapter 9).

[30]  Except, of course, where a company is in severe economic difficulties

120

which may lead it to appeal for assistance to the government. But governments are selective in their response to such appeals.

[31] The CPSA had made such a request in November 1972. Along with NUPE and the NUT, it organised a conference in February 1973, which was recognised by the TUC on an informal basis (*TUC Report 1973*, p. 290).

[32] *Economic Policy and Collective Bargaining*, Report of the Special Trades Union Congress, March 1973 (TUC, London 1973), p. 83.

[33] Ibid.

[34] *TUC Report 1973*, pp. 283–88.

[35] After an emergency meeting of the General Council on 15 October 1973, a statement was issued which concluded that 'the government has not put forward its proposals with any real intention of reaching an accommodation or understanding with the trade union movement' ('Chronicle' *British Journal of Industrial Relations*, March 1974).

[36] Strictly speaking, the legislation under which Stage Three was introduced was not formally repealed until the end of July and some of the provisions of the legislation (e.g. threshold agreements) continued for their originally intended term, but once the Conservative Party had left office a statutory incomes policy was dead.

[37] D.E. Butler and D. Kavanagh: *The British General Election of February 1974* (Macmillan, London 1974) pp. 29–30; see also John Grigg: 'The Downfall of Edward Heath' in *The Sunday Observer*, 31 March 1974, p. 29.

[38] Few single party governments this century have won an outright majority amongst the electorate as a whole. The Conservative Party polled 46.4 per cent of the total votes cast in June 1970.

[39] The relevant quotations on incomes are given in note 60 on p. 95.

[40] Quoted in Butler and Kavanagh, ibid., footnote 10 on p. 84.

[41] McKie and Cook, op.cit., pp. 30–1.

[42] See Butler and Kavanagh, op.cit., p. 139.

[43] Chapters 5 and 6 of Butler and Kavanagh (op.cit.) give a detailed record and assessment of the campaign. For Heath's own view of the accidental features in the campaign that damaged the Conservatives see his interview on Thames Television on 5 May 1974, a part of which is quoted in McKie and Cook, op.cit., p. 34.

[44] See *TUC Report 1973*, p. 282.

[45] Butler and Kavanagh quote a Conservative minister who said that the invitation 'smelled too much of politics' and that the feeling of Conservative ministers was that if the policy had been serious it would have 'been explored privately, not in the virtually public forum of the

NEDC' (Butler and Kavanagh, op.cit., p. 36).

[46] John Grigg: 'How Heath Was Trapped' in *The Sunday Observer*, 7 April 1974, p. 29.

[47] The TUC's own formula was: 'The General Council accept that there is a distinctive and exceptional situation in the mining industry' (*The Guardian*, 17 January 1974, p. 4).

[48] See Butler and Kavanagh, op.cit., pp. 98–9.

# Conclusions

The substance of this discussion of trade unions and interest group politics has revolved around the three major strategies used by trade unions to pursue their objectives: the relationship with the political and administrative executive; the relationship with the Labour Party; and the use of certain forms of direct action. A major aim of the study has been to examine the changes in the environment that influence trade union activity and also to look at the changes in the trade union movement that bear upon the use of the three main strategies that have been identified.

One of the major changes in the environment determining trade union activity, outlined in chapter 2 and further developed in chapter 4, has been the greatly increased attention given to the regulation of wage levels by governments during the 1960s. Both the attempt to develop a national planning mechanism (by means of the NEDC) and the voluntary and statutory wage policies adopted from 1961 onwards exemplify this concern. In more general terms, government has steadily added to its scope and responsibilities throughout the post-1945 period. Conservative governments in 1951 and 1970 were committed to reducing the level of state intervention and regulation but in both cases what success they did achieve had been reversed by the time they left office.

Three main changes in the trade union movement have influenced the unions' role as interest groups. First, considerable changes in the structure of trade unionism have taken place since 1945, and indeed since 1960 when Martin Harrison and Victor Allen made their analysis of the role of the unions. The impact of economic change has brought major contractions in a number of industrial sectors and a consequential decline in the numerical strength of some of the major TUC affiliates. Overall, however, trade unionism, particularly in the later 1960s, has managed to increase its density by organising in the areas of expanding employment including those employing a large number of non-manual workers. Although the TUC is not a perfect mirror of this change, if one examines the composition of the General Council one has some measure of the extent and rapidity of the change in the last fifteen years compared to the forty preceding years.[1]

The alteration in the composition of the General Council is itself evidence of the second main change in the trade union movement, for it reflects a willingness to engage in self-examination both of the structure and purposes of contemporary trade unionism. The self-examination did not lead to sufficiently extensive changes to quell many external critics of the unions and, partly in recognition of this, a Royal Commission undertook an extended inquiry into the British trade union movement between 1965 and 1968. The Commission served to prompt the trade unions and many of their external critics to further examination of the rationale of contemporary unionism.

The final kind of change that has affected the role of unions as interest groups has been the political changes in the leadership of various unions which have led to different goals being emphasised and a readiness to use strategies which were eschewed by an earlier generation of union leaders.

The cumulative impact of these changes in the environment and in the nature of trade unionism have been outlined in some detail in the previous chapters and the aim of this final chapter is therefore only to try to summarise the main direction of the argument. So far as the changes in the environment are concerned, the extension of state activities, most importantly in the area of incomes policies, has emphasised the importance of the union's relationship with the Executive. It has been successive politicians and civil servants who have been responsible for the initiation and implementation of incomes policies and the political and administrative Executive has therefore been a major pressure point for trade unions. Both in the period before the Labour Party won the 1964 Election and in the period 1972–73 discussions took place between the Party and the TUC on economic policy. In both cases, though, the nature of the 'bargain' agreed on was somewhat indeterminate so far as wage levels were concerned. This indeterminacy meant that close relationships were needed with the Labour governments of 1964 and 1974 to ensure that developments went in the direction that trade unionists desired. Given the lack of any close relationship between the Conservative Party and trade unions,[2] the importance of the relationship between the Executive and the unions was even greater.

The nature of trade union response through the TUC has been influenced by some of the organisational changes discussed below. Although trade union success in adapting to structural change in the economy has more than maintained the overall density of the movement, it has made for certain difficulties when attempting to formulate a coherent and united union position. Thus, although the affiliation of the NUT and NALGO to the TUC allowed the latter to claim an unrivalled representativeness as *the* employee organisation, it has increased the problem of achieving some operational consensus within the TUC.

Incomes policy and the attempts to change the law governing trade union activity have also had a greater impact on some unions than on others. Such a differential impact reinforced the political diversities of the trade union movement and made it difficult to agree on what constituted an acceptable incomes policy and even how to oppose what was generally agreed to be an unacceptable policy.

One of the themes that has tended to recur in the debate about incomes policies is the authority which the TUC either can or should attempt to exercise. Governments have wanted to strike bargains that will be honoured so that if they are to accept representations made by the TUC they have wanted some kind of guarantee that the General Council can ensure compliance on the part of its affiliates. Although the position of the TUC has been discussed in the internal debate within the trade union movement on the role and objectives of trade unionism, there have not been sufficient changes to allow the TUC to give guarantees on behalf of its affiliates.

But such weakness on the part of the TUC seems to have damaged its role less than one might have supposed. There seem to be two considerations which have maintained the TUC as a major interest group. In the first place it *is* the unrivalled national association of labour in Britain and, whatever its limitations, an acceptance of functional representation has dictated that continuing contacts with the TUC have been sought by government departments in connection with the wide range of matters that consultations take place on. Even where, as on incomes policy, the TUC's limitations were clear, it has remained an important medium for communicating to Whitehall the nature of union demands. Individual unions have demonstrated in relation to incomes policy, and the TUC in relation to attempts to alter the legal framework of trade union activity, that they can exercise an effective veto over the policies governments wish to pursue. The need therefore to have some idea about the price for co-operation rather than conflict is greater than ever. Such a price has frequently involved a willingness to meet other union objectives and this serves to emphasise the second factor that has maintained the TUC's credibility. Many of the subjects which have formed the basis of discussions between the TUC and the Executive have not involved the kind of commitment either by individual unions or by individual trade unionists that an incomes policy clearly did need in order to work satisfactorily. Many areas of policy are nowhere near as highly charged as incomes policy and the TUC has conducted a dialogue with various Whitehall departments which has been satisfactory to both the parties involved: the government has had its policy legitimated by engaging in the process of consulting interested parties and the TUC has had the opportunity to make progress in many of the areas with which it is concerned. The internal organisation of Congress House and the willingness to adjust its own structure[3] bear witness to the point frequently stressed by students of interest groups, namely that governmental structures exert a powerful influence over the internal structure of clientele groups.

Neither of the other major strategies discussed appear to be so important to the unions. The link with the Labour Party has remained despite all the stresses and strains of the 1960s but the changes in the trade union movement that have been outlined have had an important impact upon the relationship. The political changes in some of the major unions that were discernible in the late fifties and intensified during the following decade has meant that the leadership of the Party cannot depend upon the trade unions to support it as they did up to the middle fifties. Additionally, many of the adaptations the unions have made to the changes in the occupational structure of their membership have not followed through to the Labour Party. Major non-manual unions such as NALGO and the NUT have not followed their application to affiliate to the TUC with a similar request to the Labour Party and, although some of the most rapidly growing unions *are* formally affiliated, contracting out of the political levy is widespread.[4] The Liaison Committee established in 1972 which fathered the social contract was a body in which the unions were represented by the TUC, not through their sponsored MPs or their representatives on the NEC. It owed its existence largely to the need of the leadership of the PLP to establish a better relationship with a major interest group. Obviously, given the historical tradition in the Labour Party, the difficulties that had arisen in the period 1964–70 gave a special impetus to the need to explore the basis for a better working relationship, but the Conservative Party, after its defeats in the General Elections of 1974, had similarly to confront its failure to maintain an amicable arrangement with the unions and the implications of this failure for its existing economic and social policies.

If, as seems very likely, state financial aid is to be made available to political parties, then the structural separation of the unions and the Party will be strengthened. State aid is likely to result in an emphasis upon the political parties as the 'property' of the whole nation and to reinforce the view of the parliamentary leadership that their responsibility is to more than their own supporters – particularly as represented in the mass organisation of the political parties. The trade unions as an integral component of the Labour Party's mass organisation will be affected by this scepticism and also by the view that one of the arguments for giving state aid is to lessen the financial dependence of the two major parties on the worlds of industry and labour. Obviously if it were to be a condition of state aid that particular interests could not contribute to Party funds this would force a fundamental reconsideration of the organic link between the Party and the unions.

If some form of looser association did result from a prohibition on contributions from interested parties the unions would still have to be confronted as a major interest group. The unions' position would therefore still be an important one, particularly if one also takes into account the fact that the Labour Party would be led by those who had grown used to working within a tradition that emphasised the special relationship between the Party and the unions. Gradually, of course, those nurtured in such a tradition would cease to lead the Party and a new generation of leaders might give some further impetus to the detachment of Party and unions. It is clear that such 'detachment' is already noticeable among the generation of union leaders who have come to hold senior office in the last twenty years. In this respect they appear to reflect the characterisation of some manual workers who display more 'instrumental' or 'calculative' attitudes towards the Labour Party.[5]

The use of direct action appears to have had something of a revival in recent years. Some of its major difficulties as a viable strategy have been indicated in chapter 5. While any attempt to establish a consensual programme for action in the TUC involves difficulties, there are special problems when direct action is contemplated. Unlike relations with Whitehall departments or working through Parliament and the Labour Party, any use of direct action must be supported by the mass of the membership. As we have seen, at various points in the last five years it was made clear when direct action was under consideration by the TUC that many union members could *not* be relied upon in this respect. Nevertheless, particular unions who have been able to rely on the support of most of their members have shown that objectives can be attained through the use of direct action (e.g. the miners), and that if a particular union acts in a 'vanguard' role it may help to strengthen the case that is being made by the TUC through the use of more customary processes (e.g. the AUEW in relation to the Industrial Relations Act).

One of the difficulties direct action raised for both the trade union leadership and many of the rank and file was the distinction that was drawn between industrial and political matters and the reluctance to employ direct action techniques familiar in the former but rare in the latter. It was argued in chapter 2 that the growing concern of governments with the level of wage settlements during the 1960s has served to politicise matters previously regarded as industrial and thus only the concern of the bargaining agents, the employers and the employees. This kind of development obviously threatens the divisions between political and industrial matters as conventionally understood and if there is a lack of agreement on the re-drawing of the boundaries conflict becomes very likely. Both the miners' strikes in recent years, the 1974 strike much more clearly than that of 1972, illustrate the kind of situation that is likely to occur when a union finds itself obstructed in its wage bargaining by government-determined limits. It is impossible to say how far these events have already undermined the traditional understandings on political and industrial matters among trade unionists; thus it is very hard to guess at the future potential which these events may have unleashed.

The campaigns against the reform of industrial relations in 1969 and 1970–73 also witnessed the use of direct action. One might argue that although the campaigns were quite explicitly political, directed at preventing or obstructing changes in the law by elected governments, they can be seen more as self-contained episodes, not as having established precedents for the use of direct action on other matters. The trade unions have always concerned themselves with their legal situation since it provides the basic parameters which govern their activities. Although the position established by the 1906 and 1913 Acts was modified by the 1927 Act, this change followed a General Strike, the result of which was a testament to the weakness rather than the strength of trade unionism. The Act in 1946 which restored the position established by the pre-First World War Acts has come to be seen as the irreducible minimum for the functioning of trade unions. Any direct attack upon it – as the 1969 proposals and the 1971 Act were seen as being – were consequently bound to be strongly resisted. Such resistance has given the trade unions a strong bargaining position in other areas of policy in which they are interested.

The final limitation that seems to attach to the use of direct action as it has so far manifested itself, is its negative or veto aspect. It has been used to frustrate and obstruct the desires of governments but not consciously to further the positive objectives of trade unionists. In other words it has worked to defend the trade unions' existing position, for example, in relation to maintaining the existing legal position, but not to advance beyond these statutes. Governments have responded by asking the trade unions how such veto action can be avoided since they are concerned at the damage it brings about. Indirectly, therefore, it certainly has provided the backdrop to both the tripartite talks and the social contract. The major problem for trade unions, particularly for the TUC, in operating in a veto capacity is that it does not succeed in disposing of the problems that governments have seen themselves as being faced with. Consequently, governments have resorted to other policies in order to solve these problems since certain preferred solutions have been closed off by trade union action.

The clearest examples of this resort to other policies are deflation and unemployment. The trade unions are opposed to both but have not yet devised a means to ensure that they are avoided as policy choices by governments. Both Labour and Conservative governments since 1945 have recognised that Britain has to operate within an international economy and that this greatly inhibits and constrains their range of policy choices. One can argue that the abandonment of some policy goals generally agreed on by governments since 1945 might create more freedom to maneouvre but many of the basic facts about the British economy can only be modified over a long time scale. Thus there is no short term possibility of reducing the dependence upon imported food and raw materials.[6] The need to import in turn creates a need to maximise the volume and the value of exported manufactured goods. If trade unions succeed in achieving rises in money wages which are in excess of the increases in productivity, then it is impossible to avoid a deterioration in the prospects for exported goods.[7] If an incomes policy which aims at linking the growth of incomes to improvements in productivity is rejected, then unemployment is likely to result unless the government is willing to take further counter-action.

Such counter-action can take a number of forms: trade unions have normally urged that governments should stimulate the economy, utilising the customary range of fiscal measures. Governments have regularly shown themselves responsive to such suggestions but this has not prevented unemployment totals far in excess of what trade unions thought tolerable. The difficulties of a viable incomes policy are now seen as so great that the former hope of protecting employment in return for incomes restraint appears less and less credible to many politicians. If free collective bargaining is to be maintained then its likely concomitant is seen as a much higher level of unemployment.

Possibly as a reaction to this trade unionists have come to emphasise the notion of job protection and some localised manifestations of direct action have been explicitly directed towards this end. Such a response has found some support among sections of the 1974 Labour government, though one cannot be very optimistic about such support for it is by no means equally evident among all members of the government. Further-

129

more, unemployment is likely to accumulate more by non-replacement of those retiring and leaving companies, by a restriction on recruitment (e.g. on school leavers) and by partial shedding of labour rather than wholesale plant closures. It is also clear that where the State is willing to provide finance for firms that are ailing and thus to prolong employment, there will be a price to be paid in terms of a close scrutiny of all aspects of the current structure and functioning of such companies. Such a scrutiny will involve many matters which vitally affect trade unionists and it is most unlikely that they will emerge unscathed at the end of the enquiry (the inquiry into British Leyland is instructive in this respect).

The greater part of the discussion in this book has been devoted to an examination of the experience of trade unions as interest groups in the last fifteen years. Already in the remarks in the preceding paragraph we have begun to stray into a prediction of the future pattern of events. As a conclusion to this discussion it is worthwhile to try to sketch out a number of alternative scenarios which may offer some clues as to the likely future course of events.

The first of these might be labelled the 'corporatist' model. So far as the full-time staff of the TUC are concerned it is clear that there is a very narrow line that divides incorporation as part of the machinery of government from a close relationship with, but still recognisable separation from, government. The last three General Secretaries have all been anxious to maintain an independent position for the trade union movement, but equally to maximise the opportunities for exercising influence: 'driving a series of bargains with the government, but not becoming an agent of the State'.[8] The influence of the Secretaries and Presidents who comprise the General Council is probably to strengthen the emphasis on maintaining a recognisably independent position. Nevertheless, as Pahl and Winkler[9] have argued persuasively, a number of important developments can be seen as pushing British society and politics in a corporatist direction and trade unions may find it extremely difficult to stand out clearly against these trends.[10] In the light of Britain's economic position in the middle 1970s, there is a real prospect of a decline in living standards and substantial levels of unemployment. There must be a considerable temptation to strike a bargain with the government which will minimise the impact of these prospects. But such a bargain is only likely to be forthcoming on the government's part if the unions show a willingness to sacrifice or substantially attenuate some important right that they now possess. One possibility of this kind would be an agreement on the indexation of wages in return for certain guarantees directed towards maintaining full employment and, perhaps more generally,

130

maintaining certain levels of public expenditure.

It is true that such an arrangement would seem to undermine part of the logic of trade unionism but if the dimensions of economic crisis are more severe than anything experienced since the 1930s, then although old habits and responses die hard, they may eventually die. If the signs that the social contract is not producing the required level of wage restraint continue to accumulate, the General Council will not be in a strong position to argue for the efficacy of self-restraint. It may then find it possible to take part in the administration of an index-linked pay system interpreted with some flexibility but basically deriving from and enforced by a government-provided legal framework. One major difficulty for any General Council tempted by such an arrangement will be fears about the consequences for trade union membership. One likely consequence of corporatism would be a reduced ability to respond to rank and file demands and thus to increase the possibility of disaffection and the potential for breakaway unions.

Precisely because of these kinds of risks it may be more plausible to argue for a second scenario which for want of a better term can be labelled 'muddling through'. It assumes that even if an incorporative arrangement is offered it will be rejected by the trade unions. As the term 'muddling through' implies, nothing would change very radically as regards the role of trade unions. It suggests that heavier unemployment and a reduction in living standards, although strongly criticised, will be tolerated mainly in the expectation that they would be strictly temporary. The hope would be that once North Sea oil is landed in Britain there would be a return to (relative) prosperity and full employment. If one adds that this scenario assumes the retention of free collective bargaining then it must appear highly plausible. Not only does free collective bargaining preserve the role of the unions in the determination of wages, it also enables some unions to actually advance their members' interests despite economic depression and unemployment. While many trade unionists' wage levels may be stationary or declining, unions who represent workers in key strategic areas can do rather better than this. Economists and politicians may tell them that they are only able to insist on a particular wage at the expense of other workers but there is little evidence that such warnings will restrain them. Hence the fact that even in conditions of unemployment and high inflation it is possible for some groups to improve their situation and probably for many more to deceive themselves that they are doing so, inhibits any general trade union agreement especially if it involves some sacrifice of free collective bargaining. This is a further reason for having doubts about the first

131

scenario, at any rate insofar as it involves a generalised response from trade unions articulated through the TUC.

There is a third scenario which ought to be considered, and which can be dubbed the 'radical' possibility. This scenario derives from the radicalising potential of statutory incomes control. We have already noted the way in which such controls made divisions between the industrial and the political difficult to maintain. In an address to the British Association in 1969 John Goldthorpe accepted the arguments of those who have stressed the existence of a wide consensus on political arrangements in Britain. But he argued that this had tended to ignore the significance of widespread industrial unrest as an indication of the lack of any consensus on justifiable inequalities in this country. Contrary to the intentions of those who had introduced statutory controls, the attempt to demonstrate a rational justification for inequalities would be more likely to do the opposite:

> . . . through increasing information about, and interest in, differences between occupational rewards and conditions, the actual operations of an incomes policy will serve to broaden comparative reference groups among the mass of the population and at the same time bring issues of equity and fairness into greater subjective salience.[11]

He does not himself go on to speculate whether the absence of normative agreement on rewards in society has the potential to break down the insulation of the political system from industrial discontent. But in statutory pay policies the government appears as the arbiter of rewards and there does seem a possible basis for dissatisfaction to spread since if the kind of rewards the government is specifying are seen as unfair then the political processes by which it comes to such decisions may in turn be questioned. Even if statutory incomes policy does not return, the spectacle of a government either refusing to boost the economy sufficiently to ensure continuing employment or cutting public expenditure on a large scale might cause a sufficiently great jolt to conventional expectations to produce a radical response from trade unionists. How far the trade union leadership would reflect and articulate such a radical response is uncertain. Although many trade unions are nominally committed to alternative social and political orders there is little sign that many trade union leaders have thought much about the implications of such a commitment, particularly about the appropriate means to reach such alternative goals.

The three scenarios that have been sketched out above have been developed by extrapolating particular aspects of the behaviour of interest groups identified in this book. It would be a brave, and probably foolish, student of trade unions who was prepared to assert emphatically that any one was overwhelmingly plausible. There are obviously other scenarios that could be outlined, possibly far more plausible than those discussed above. It is possible that someone writing a similar book to this in 1970 would have felt able to predict events such as the two miners' strikes, the resistance to the Industrial Relations Act 1971, and the Arab—Israeli War of October 1973 which brought the oil crisis in its wake. But simply to list these events is to show the inherent unlikelihood of such a prediction and we have tried to demonstrate in our discussion of the trade unions and their strategies that these events have been of great importance. It is therefore difficult to conclude on other than a tentative and circumspect note.

## Notes

[1] The General Council is divided into a number of trade groups with representation according to union size. Between 1921 and 1961 one new group was created and there were three changes in the representation given to the remaining groups. Between 1961 and 1973 two entirely new groups were created, four of the existing groups were amalgamated to give two new groups, and seven changes were made in the representation given to the remaining groups.

[2] The Party does have a Trade Union Advisory Committee but it attracts individual trade unionists sympathetic to the Conservative Party rather than trade unions as organisations.

[3] The TUC, in embarking on the establishment of a regional framework for its activities, stressed the extent to which it was influenced by trends to decentralisation on the part of central government and the re-organisation of local government. It is also worth noting that one of the two broad tasks given to the re-organised machinery was 'the pressure group function' (*TUC Report 1973*, pp. 356 and 358).

[4] For example, ASTMS (see Richter, op cit., p. 183). Bain comments generally that among white-collar unions who affiliate to the Labour Party 'their contracting-out rates are generally higher than those of manual unions' (Bain, op cit. [1970], p. 115).

[5] The discussion of the 'affluent' worker is one of the best known documentations of these attitudes; see J.H. Goldthorpe et al.: *The Affluent Worker in the Class Structure* (Cambridge University Press, London 1969).

133

[6] The enormous attention given to the possibilities of North Sea oil as a means of saving on the import bill is an illustration of this reliance.

[7] Unless the inflationary rates in other countries which are competing with Britain are greater — which in recent years has not been the case in general.

[8] A description of Len Murray's attitude. Murray himself said: 'We can never be the agents of a political party — or of the State' in 'A Two-Way Talk with Len Murray' (*The Director*, June 1974).

[9] R.E. Pahl and J.T. Winkler: 'The Coming Corporatism' (*New Society*, 19 October 1974).

[10] Indeed, as has been noted in the discussion of the NEDC in chapter 4, the TUC has been an important contributor to the development of corporatist solutions to problems.

[11] J.H. Goldthorpe: 'Social Inequality and Social Integration in Modern Britain', originally in *Advancement of Science*, vol. 26, December 1969, reprinted in D.C. Wedderburn (ed.): *Poverty, Inequality and Class Structure* (Cambridge University Press, London 1974).

# Bibliography

Allen, V.L.: *Trade Union Leadership* (Longman, London 1957).

Allen, V.L.: *Trade Unions and the Government* (Longman, London 1960).

Allen, V.L.: *The Sociology of Industrial Relations* (Longman, London 1970).

Allen, V.L.: 'The Re-organisation of the Trades Union Congress 1918–1927' (*British Journal of Sociology,* vol. 11, 1960).

Attlee, G.R.: *The Labour Party in Perspective* (Gollancz, London, 1937).

Bain, G.S.: *The Growth of White Collar Unionism* (Oxford University Press, London 1970).

Bain, G.S.: 'The Growth of White Collar Unionism in Great Britain' (*British Journal of Industrial Relations,* vol. 4 [3], November 1966).

Bains, G.S. and Clegg, H.A.: 'A Strategy for Industrial Relations Research in Great Britain' (*British Journal of Industrial Relations,* vol. 12 [1], March 1974).

Bain, G.S. and Price, R.: 'Union Growth and Employment Trends in the UK' (*British Journal of Industrial Relations,* vol. 10 [3], November 1972).

Bain, G.S. and Woolven, G.B.: 'The Primary Materials of British Industrial Relations' (*British Journal of Industrial Relations,* vol. 9 [3], November 1971).

Banks, J.A.: *Trade Unionism* (Collier Macmillan, London 1974).

Barker, A. and Rush, M.: *The Member of Parliament and his Information* (George Allen and Unwin, London 1970).

Beer, S.H.: *Modern British Politics* (Faber, London 1965).

Benewick, R. and Smith, T. (eds): *Direct Action and Democratic Politics* (George Allen and Unwin, London 1972).

Bentley, A.: *The Process of Government* (Harvard University Press, 1971).

Bing, I. (ed.): *The Labour Party: An Organisational Study* (Fabian Society, London 1971).

Birch, Lionel: *The History of the TUC 1868–1968* (Trades Union Congress, London 1968).

Birkenhead, Lord: *Walter Monckton* (Weidenfeld and Nicolson, London 1969).

Blackaby, Frank (ed.): *An Incomes Policy for Britain* (Heinemann, London 1973).

135

Brittan, S.: *The Treasury Under the Tories* (Penguin, Harmondsworth 1964).

Butler, D.E. and Kavanagh, D.: *The British General Election of February 1974* (Macmillan, London 1974).

Butler, D.E. and Pinto-Duschinsky, M.: *The British General Election of 1970* (Macmillan, London 1971).

Butler D.E. and Stokes, D.E.: *Political Change in Britain* (Macmillan, London 1969).

Calder, A.: *The People's War* (Jonathan Cape, London 1969).

Carter, A.: *Direct Action and Liberal Democracy* (Routledge and Kegan Paul, London 1973).

Castles, F.G.: *Pressure Groups and Political Culture* (Routledge and Kegan Paul, London 1967).

Citrine, Lord: *Men and Work* (Hutchinson, London 1964).

Clegg, H.A.: *How to Run an Incomes Policy and Why We Made Such a Mess of the Last One* (Heinemann, London 1971).

Clegg, H.A.: *The System of Industrial Relations in Britain* (Basil Blackwell, Oxford 1972).

Clegg, H.A., Fox, A. and Thompson, A.F.: *A History of British Trade Unions Since 1889*, vol. 1 1889–1910 (Oxford University Press, London 1964).

Coates, R.D.: *Teachers Unions and Interest Group Politics* (Cambridge University Press, London 1972).

Cole, G.D.H.: *Short History of the British Working Class Movement* (George Allen and Unwin, London, first edition 1927, second edition, 1948).

Corina, J.: *The Labour Market: Part One of Incomes Policy, Problems and Prospects* (Institute of Personnel Management, London 1966).

Craig, F.W.S.: *British General Election Manifesto, 1918–66* (Political Reference Publications, Chichester 1970).

Crewe, I., Sarlvik, B. and Alt, J.: 'The Why and How of the February Voting' *(New Society,* 12 September 1974*).*

Dorfman, G.A.: *Wage Politics in Britain* (Charles Knight, London 1974).

Edinger, L.J. and Searing, D.D.: *'Social Background in Elite Analysis' (American Political Science Review,* vol. 61 [2], June 1967).

Ellis, John and Johnson, R.W.: *Members from the Unions* (Fabian Society, London 1974).

*Fair Deal at Work* (Conservative Party, London 1968).

Finer, S.E.: *Anonymous Empire* (Pall Mall, London 1958).

Finer, S.E.: 'The Federation of British Industries' *(Political Studies,* vol. 4 [1], February 1956).

Fisher, N.: *Iain Macleod* (Deutsch, London 1973).

Ghosh, S.C.: 'Decision Making and Power in the British Conservative Party' (*Political Studies,* vol. 13[2], June 1965).

Goldthorpe, J.H., Lockwood, D., Bechhofer F. and Platt J.: *The Affluent Worker: Political Behaviour* (Cambridge University Press, London 1968).

Goldthorpe, J.H., Lockwood D., Bechhofer F. and Platt, J.: *The Affluent Worker in the Class Structure* (Cambridge University Press, London 1969).

Goldthorpe, J.H.: 'Social Inequality and Social Integration in Modern Britain' (*Advancement of Science,* vol. 26, December 1969).

Grant, W.P. and Marsh, D.: 'The Confederation of British Industry' (*Political Studies,* vol. 19, October 1971).

Grant, W.P. and Marsh, D.: 'The Politics of the CBI: 1974 and After' (*Government and Opposition,* vol. 10[1], Winter 1975).

Grigg, John: 'The Downfall of Edward Heath' (*The Observer,* 31 March 1974).

Grigg, John: 'How Heath was Trapped' (*The Observer,* 7 April 1974).

Guttsman, W.E.: *The British Political Elite* (Macgibbon and Kee, London 1963).

Hanby, Victor: 'A Changing Labour Elite: The National Executive Committee of the Labour Party 1900–1972' in I. Crewe (ed.): *British Political Sociology Year Book,* vol. 1 (Croom Helm, London 1974).

Heffer, E.S.: *The Class Struggle in Parliament* (Gollancz, London 1973).

Houghton, D.: 'Trade Union MPs in the House of Commons' (*The Parliamentarian,* vol. 44[4], October 1968).

*House of Lords Weekly Hansard,* no. 900, cols. 1020–47.

Hughes, John and Pollins, H.: *Trade Unions in Great Britain* (David and Charles, Newton Abbot 1973).

Ingham, G.K.: *Strikes and Industrial Conflict* (Macmillan, London 1974).

Jacobs, E.: 'Jack Jones, Leader of the Labour Party' (*The Sunday Times,* 1 September 1974).

Jenkins, P.: *The Battle of Downing Street* (Charles Knight, London 1970).

Jones, A.: *The New Inflation* (Penguin, Harmondsworth 1975).

Jones, C.: 'Paying the Pipers to Play the Tune' (*The Financial Times,* 3 August 1974).

Lane, T.: *The Union Makes Us Strong* (Arrow, London 1974).

McCarthy, W.E.J.: *The Future of the Unions* (Fabian Society, London 1962).

McKenzie, R.T.: *British Political Parties* Heinemann, London 1955).

McKie, D. and Cook, C.: *The Guardian/Quartet Election Guide* (Quartet Books, London 1974).

McKenzie, W.J.M.: 'Pressure Groups in British Government' (*British Journal of Sociology,* vol. 4[2], 1955).

Macmillan, H.: *At the End of the Day* (Macmillan, London 1973).

Milne Bailey, W.: *Trade Unions and the State* (George Allen and Unwin, London 1934).

Muller, W.P.: 'Trade Union Sponsored Members of Parliament in the Defence Dispute of 1960–61' (*Parliamentary Affairs,* vol. 23 [3], Summer 1970).

Muller, W.P.: 'Union/MP Conflict: An Overview' (*Parliamentary Affairs,* vol. 26 [3], Summer 1973).

Muller, W.P.: *The Parliamentary Activities of Trade Union MPs 1959–1964'* (unpublished Ph.D., University of Florida 1966).

Pahl, R.E. and Winkler, J.T.: 'The Coming Corporatism' (*New Society,* 10 October 1974).

Panitch, L.: 'Ideology and Integration: The Case of the British Labour Party (*Political Studies,* vol. 19[2], June 1971).

Panitch, L.: *The Labour Party and the Trade Unions: A Study of Incomes Policy since 1945 with Special Reference to 1964–70* (unpublished Ph.D. thesis, University of London 1973).

*Parliamentary Debates,* 5th Series, vol. 878, col. 32.

Pelling, H.M.: *The Origins of the Labour Party* (Clarendon Press, Oxford 1965).

Pelling, H.M.: *A Short History of the Labour Party* (Macmillan, London 1961).

Pickles, W.: 'Trade Unions in the Political Climate' in B.C. Roberts (ed.): *Industrial Relations, Contemporary Problems and Perspectives* (Methuen, London, revised edition 1968).

Political and Economic Planning: *Advisory Committees in British Government* (George Allen and Unwin, London 1960).

Political and Economic Planning: *Trade Union Membership* (London 1962).

Political and Economic Planning: *Trade Unions in a Changing Society* (London 1963).

Political and Economic Planning: *The Structure and Organisation of British Trade Unions* (London 1963).

Potter, A.M.: *Organised Groups in British National Politics* (Faber, London 1961).

Price, J.T.: *Organised Labour in the War* (Penguin Books, Harmondsworth 1940).

Rawson, D.W.: 'The Life Span of Labour Parties' (*Political Studies,* vol. 17[3], October 1969).

Robertson, N. and Sams, K.: *British Trade Unionism,* vol. 1 (Basil Blackwell, Oxford, 1972).

Rose, C.R.: *Politics in England Today* (Faber, London 1974).

Rush, M.: *The Selection of Parliamentary Candidates* (Nelson, London 1969).

Simpson, D.H.: 'An Analysis of the Size of Unions' (*British Journal of Industrial Relations,* vol. 10[3], November 1972).

Simpson, W.: *Labour, the Unions and the Party* (George Allen and Unwin, London 1973).

*Socialist Commentary,* October 1965.

Stewart, M.: *Protest or Power: A Study of the Labour Party* (George Allen and Unwin, London 1974).

Trades Union Congress: *Reports of Annual Trades Union Congresses 1961–73.*

Trades Union Congress: *Trade Unionism* (London 1966).

Trades Union Congress: *Incomes Policy – Report of a Conference of Executive Committees of Affiliated Organisations,* March 1967 (London 1967).

Trades Union Congress: *The Industrial Relations Bill – Report of the Special Trades Union Congress* (London 1971).

Trades Union Congress: *Economic Policy and Collective Bargaining – Report of a Special TUC, March 1973* (London 1973).

Turner, H.A.: 'Collective Bargaining and the Eclipse of Incomes Policy: Retrospect, Prospect and Possibilities' (*British Journal of Industrial Relations,* vol. 8.

Walkland, S.A.: *The Legislative Process in Great Britain* (George Allen and Unwin, London 1968).

Webb, S. and Webb, B.: *A History of Trade Unionism* (Longmans, London 1894).

Winch, D.: *Economics and Policy* (Hodder and Stoughton, London 1969).

Vaughan, G.D.: 'Economic Development Committees' (*Public Administration,* vol. 49, Winter 1971).

Volker, D.: 'NALGO's Affiliation to the TUC' (*British Journal of Industrial Relations,* vol 4[1], March, 1966).

# Index

Indexer's note: certain references in the index may lead to chapter note indices; where the reader is unable to find the subject from the page reference given, he should turn to the notes at the end of the chapter for the necessary lead. Explanation of the acronyms used will be found in the glossary on pages 146 and 147.

White-collar workers, special problems of 86, 96

Wilberforce recommendations 115

Williamson 26

Willis, Bob 83

Wilson, J. Harold, 25–7, 35–6, 40–1, 56, 100–1, 118

Woodcock, George 6, 36, 69–72, 85, 87, 89

Young Socialists 38

# Glossary

| | |
|---|---|
| ACTT | Association of Cinematograph, Television and Allied Technicians |
| AUEW | Amalgamated Union of Engineering Workers (formerly AEF and AEU) |
| APEX | Association of Professional, Executive Clerical and Computer Staff (formerly CAWU) |
| ASTMS | Association of Scientific, Technical and Managerial Staffs |
| ATTI | Association of Teachers in Technical Institutions |
| BMA | British Medical Association |
| CAWU | Clerical and Administrative Workers Union (now APEX) |
| CBI | Confederation of British Industry |
| CLP | Constituency Labour Party |
| COHSE | Confederation of Health Service Employees |
| CPSA | Civil and Public Services Association |
| DATA | Draughtsmen and Allied Technicians Association (now TASS) |
| DEA | Department of Economic Affairs |
| EDC | Economic Development Committee |
| EETU/PTU | Electrical, Electronic Telecommunication and Plumbing Union |
| ETU | Electrical Trades Union (now EETU/PTU) |
| GLC | Greater London Council |
| LPACR | Labour Party Annual Conference Report |
| LRC | Labour Representation Committee |
| NALGO | National Association of Local Government Officers |
| NEC | National Executive Committee of the Labour Party |
| NEDC | National Economic Development Council |
| NIC | National Incomes Commission |
| NIRC | National Industrial Relations Court |
| NUBE | National Union of Bank Employees |
| NUGMW | Nation Union of General and Municipal Workers |
| NUM | National Union of Mineworkers |
| NUPE | National Union of Public Employees |
| NUR | National Union of Railwaymen |
| NUT | National Union of Teachers |

| | |
|---|---|
| PEP | Political and Economic Planning |
| PLP | Parliamentary Labour Party |
| POEU | Post Office Engineering Union |
| TASS | Technical and Supervisory Section of AUEW (formerly DATA) |
| TGWU | Transport and General Workers Union |
| TSSA | Transport Salaried Staffs' Association |
| TUC | Trades Union Congress |
| UCATT | Union of Construction Allied Trades and Technicians |
| UPW | Union of Post Office Workers |
| USDAW | Union of Shop, Distributive and Allied Workers |

# The Author

Timothy May graduated in Sociology and Politics from the University of Leeds. He has carried out research into the youth organisations of British political parties and from 1964 to 1967 was Organising Tutor for the Worker's Educational Association. In 1967 he was appointed Senior Lecturer in Politics at Manchester Polytechnic.

J3